AGS® *Reading Skills for Life*

Level P

AGS®

American Guidance Service, Inc.
Circle Pines, Minnesota 55014-1796
1-800-328-2560

Content Reviewers

The publisher wishes to thank the following educators for their helpful guidance and review during the development process for *Reading Skills for Life.* Their assistance has been invaluable.

Jack Cassidy, Ph.D.
Professor of Education
Texas A&M University
Corpus Christi, Texas

James Johnston
Reading Specialist
Portsmouth High School
Portsmouth, New Hampshire

Alva Webb Jones, Ed.S.
Special Education Consultant
Richmond County Board of Education
Augusta, Georgia

Robin Pence
Reading Specialist
Clay High School
Clay County Schools
Green Cove Springs, FL

Ted Stuff
School Psychologist
Special Education
    Department Chair
McLaughlin High School
Anchorage, Alaska

Development and editorial services provided by Straight Line Editorial Development, Inc.

Photo and Illustration Credits

Pages 7, 18 (top, middle, bottom), 22, 26, 30, Sandy Rabinowitz; pp. 8, 9,12, 13, 16, 17, 20, 24, 25, 33, 38, 46, 50, 63, 68 (all) Judy King; pp. 10, 14 (all) Donald Cook; pp. 37, 40 (left, right), 44, 48, 52, 67, 70, 82, 90, Joel Snyder; p. 56 (top, bottom), © Superstock/ Superstock International; pp. 56 (middle), 60 (top left), © Galen Rowell/ Corbis; p. 60 (top right), © GEORGE F. MOBLEY/ National Geographic Image Collection; p. 60 (bottom left), © Ed Webster/ Mountain Imagery/ The American Alpine Club; p. 60 (bottom right), © Spectrum Stock, Inc./ Spectrum Stock; p. 74, © Paula Illingworth/ AP Wide World Photos; p. 86 (left), © Jim Chatwin/ Index Stock Imagery; p. 86 (middle), © Todd Powell/ Index Stock Imagery; p. 86 (right), © Brigitte Lambert/ Image Bank; pp. 97, 101, 106, 124, 130, 141, 145, 151, 163, 168, Roberta Collier-Morales; pp. 112, 113 (all) © joyrides.com/ Joyrides.com; p. 118, © NASA/ NASA Media Resource Center

Publisher's Project Staff

Director, Product Development: Karen Dahlen; Associate Director, Product Development: Teri Mathews; Editor: Jody Peterson; Development Assistant: Bev Johnson; Designer and Cover Illustrator: Denise Bunkert; Design Manager: Nancy Condon; Desktop Publishing Specialist: Linda Peterson; Desktop Publishing Manager: Lisa Beller; Purchasing Agent: Mary Kaye Kuzma; Executive Director of Marketing: Matt Keller; Marketing Manager: Brian Holl

Printed in the United States of America

ISBN 0-7854-2647-7

Product Number 91750

A 0 9 8 7 6 5 4 3

CONTENTS

◆ Word Study Tips 6

◆ Chapter 1 7

   Lesson 1 "The Bungee Jump," Part 1 8

   Lesson 2 "The Bungee Jump," Part 2 12

   Lesson 3 "The Cave," Part 1 16

   Lesson 4 "The Cave," Part 2 20

   Lesson 5 "At the Water Slide," Part 1 24

   Lesson 6 "At the Water Slide," Part 2 28

             Summary of Skills and Strategies 32

             Chapter 1 Review 33

◆ Chapter 2 37

   Lesson 1 "Paddle and Roll," Part 1 38

   Lesson 2 "Paddle and Roll," Part 2 42

   Lesson 3 "The Track," Part 1 46

   Lesson 4 "The Track," Part 2 50

   Lesson 5 "Go Climb a Rock" 54

   Lesson 6 "Big Walls!" 58

             Summary of Skills and Strategies 62

             Chapter 2 Review 63

◆ Chapter 3 67

   Lesson 1 "Kick-It-Back" 68

   Lesson 2 "The Sub Comes Up" 72

   Lesson 3 "Airplane Quiz" 76

   Lesson 4 "Night Jump!" 80

   Lesson 5 "Karate" 84

   Lesson 6 "Karate Cool" 88

             Summary of Skills and Strategies 92

             Chapter 3 Review 93

◆ **Chapter 4** 97

    Lesson 1 "In Costume," Part 1 98

    Lesson 2 "In Costume," Part 2 104

    Lesson 3 "America's Biggest and Baddest Rides" 110

    Lesson 4 "Girls Send Plastics Into Space" 116

    Lesson 5 "Take It by Skate," Part 1 122

    Lesson 6 "Take It by Skate," Part 2 128

           Summary of Skills and Strategies 134

           Chapter 4 Review 135

◆ **Chapter 5** 141

    Lesson 1 "Up in Smoke," Part 1 142

    Lesson 2 "Up in Smoke," Part 2 148

    Lesson 3 "What Are You Putting in Your Body?" 154

    Lesson 4 "Beep Me!" Part 1 160

    Lesson 5 "Beep Me!" Part 2 166

    Lesson 6 "Number Games" 172

           Summary of Skills and Strategies 178

           Chapter 5 Review 179

Word Bank 185

◆ Welcome!

Reading is like anything else that matters. In order to be good at it, you have to practice.

Here is how *Reading Skills for Life* will help you become a better reader:

▶ **You will learn the sounds that letters stand for.** Knowing the sounds letters stand for lets you figure out new words by sounding them out.

▶ **You will get to know important words by sight.** Some words can't be sounded out. You just have to remember the way they look. Knowing lots of words by sight is one big key to reading.

▶ **You will know how words can change.** This book will help you see how words change, and what the changes mean.

▶ **You will read better by reading more.** You will read stories about characters who face real-life problems and find solutions. You will also learn some facts about the real world. (Some of these may surprise you!) And you will read about some real people who have done amazing things.

▶ **You will learn about yourself.** Your ideas are important! This book will help you think about what you read. What **you** think about what you read matters. This book gives you plenty of chances to "be the judge."

With a little practice, you'll be reading like a pro in no time! So start reading!

◆ The Five Steps to Learning a Word

1. **Read the word.** Notice its shape. Is it long or short? What letters does it begin with? Does it look like other words you know?

2. **Say the word.** What sounds does it have? Which letters stand for those sounds?

3. **Write the word.** Get a feel for the word by writing it down.

4. **Add the word to your Word Bank.** You will find a Word Bank in the back of this book. It has space for you to write the new words you learn. Your Word Bank lets you keep track of all the words you are learning.

5. **Practice reading the word.** Read the word again and again until you know it.

◆ Tips for Reading Longer Words

Short words are usually simple to read. It's easy to get stumped when you come to longer words. Here are some tips that can help:

Look for word parts you know. Is the word made up of a smaller word you know, plus an ending?

Look for letter patterns you know. If you know one pattern of letters, like the **ain** in **main,** use it when you come to other words. Knowing **main** can help you read lots of words you may not know, such as **pain, train, stained,** and **raining.**

Break the word into parts. Is the word made up of two smaller words that have been put together?

Look for syllables. The vowels in a word are a clue to how many syllables it has.

Think about the sounds the letters stand for. Look at the letters in the word. What sounds do the letters stand for? Blend all the sounds together to read the word.

CHAPTER 1

Lesson 1 . . . . page 8
"The Bungee Jump," Part 1

Lesson 2 . . . . page 12
"The Bungee Jump," Part 2

Lesson 3 . . . . page 16
"The Cave," Part 1

Lesson 4 . . . . page 20
"The Cave," Part 2

Lesson 5 . . . . page 24
"At the Water Slide," Part 1

Lesson 6 . . . . page 28
"At the Water Slide," Part 2

Letters and Sounds

◆ **Directions:** Look at the letter at the beginning of each line. Then say the name of each picture. If the word begins with that letter, write the letter on the line.

m	f	s

m

1. _____   2. _____   3. _____

f

4. _____   5. _____   6. _____

s

7. _____   8. _____   9. _____

◆ **Directions:** Say the name of each picture. Circle the letter it begins with.

10. **s m f**   11. **m f s**   12. **f s m**

Word Bank

Each of these story words appears in the Word Bank at the back of this book.

Story Words

◆ **Directions:** Read each word to yourself. Then say the word out loud. Write the word on the line. Check the box after each step.

I	Read ❑ Say ❑ Write ❑ _____
make	Read ❑ Say ❑ Write ❑ _____
can	Read ❑ Say ❑ Write ❑ _____
a	Read ❑ Say ❑ Write ❑ _____
said	Read ❑ Say ❑ Write ❑ _____
yes	Read ❑ Say ❑ Write ❑ _____
you	Read ❑ Say ❑ Write ❑ _____
may	Read ❑ Say ❑ Write ❑ _____
will	Read ❑ Say ❑ Write ❑ _____
no	Read ❑ Say ❑ Write ❑ _____
not	Read ❑ Say ❑ Write ❑ _____
the	Read ❑ Say ❑ Write ❑ _____
bungee (bun | gee)	Read ❑ Say ❑ Write ❑ _____
jump	Read ❑ Say ❑ Write ❑ _____
fall	Read ❑ Say ❑ Write ❑ _____
snap	Read ❑ Say ❑ Write ❑ _____

More Word Work

◆ **Directions:** Find a story word that begins with the same letter as each picture. Write it under the picture.

13. _____   14. _____   15. _____

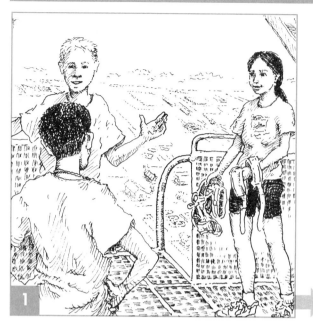

THE BUNGEE JUMP, PART 1

Matt said, "I can bungee jump. Can you?"

Sam said, "Yes, I can jump."

"OK," said Matt. "Jump!"

"3, 2, 1," said Sam. "No, I can not jump. I may fall."

"Sam," said Matt, "you will not fall. Make the jump."

"No," said Sam. "The bungee may snap. You make the jump."

"OK," said Matt, "I will. The bungee will not snap."

"OK," said Sam, "Jump."

"Yes, I can jump," said Matt,

"OK," said Sam. "3, 2, 1—"

"BUNGEE!" said Matt.

What Do You Think?

◆ 1. Would you ever bungee jump? Circle your answer.

YES   **NO**

2. Why or why not? Check one reason, or write your own.

❏ like thrills   ❏ don't like heights

❏ could be fun   ❏ too dangerous

_____ (your own reason)

3. Write a sentence telling why you would or would not bungee jump.

_____

_____

_____

Think About the Story

Use Story Words

◆ **Directions:** Write a word from the box to finish each sentence.

snap	make	fall	jump	bungee

4. Matt said, "I can _____ jump."

5. Sam said, "I can not _____."

6. Sam said, "I may _____."

7. "I will _____ the jump," said Matt.

8. Matt said, "The bungee will not _____."

When Did It Happen?

◆ 9. Write a number from 1 to 5 in front of each event to show when it happened.

_____ Sam said, "You make the jump."

_____ "Yes, I can jump," said Sam.

_____ "BUNGEE!" said Matt.

_____ "I will make the jump," said Matt.

_____ Matt said, "I can bungee jump. Can you?"

Letters and Sounds

◆ **Directions:** Look at the letter at the beginning of each line. Then say the name of each picture. If the word begins with that letter, write the letter on the line.

t	n	r

t

1. _____   2. _____   3. _____

n

4. _____   5. _____   6. _____

r

7. _____   8. _____   9. _____

◆ **Directions:** Say the name of each picture. Circle the letter it begins with.

10. **t   n   r**   11. **r   t   n**   12. **n   r   t**

Story Words

◆ **Directions:** Read each word to yourself. Then say the word out loud. Write the word on the line. Check the box after each step.

up	Read ❑ Say ❑ Write ❑ _____
to	Read ❑ Say ❑ Write ❑ _____
get	Read ❑ Say ❑ Write ❑ _____
for	Read ❑ Say ❑ Write ❑ _____
did	Read ❑ Say ❑ Write ❑ _____
down	Read ❑ Say ❑ Write ❑ _____
went	Read ❑ Say ❑ Write ❑ _____
ran	Read ❑ Say ❑ Write ❑ _____
off	Read ❑ Say ❑ Write ❑ _____

◆ **Directions:** Find a story word that begins with the same letter as each picture. Write it under the picture.

13. _____   14. _____   15. _____

More Word Work

◆ **Directions:** Write a word from the box to fit each clue.

no	can	down

16. not "yes"   _____

17. not "up"   _____

18. may   _____

THE BUNGEE JUMP, PART 2

The bungee went down, up, down, up, down.

Matt went down, up, down, up, down.

Did the bungee snap? No!

"Sam," said Matt. "Will you jump?"

"OK, OK," said Sam. "Yes, I will."

"3, 2, 1," said Matt. "Jump off!"

"BUNGEE!" said Sam. The bungee went down, up, down, up, down.

Sam went down, up, down, up, down.

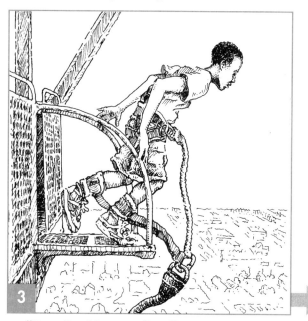

Rama ran up to Matt.

"I will get the bungee off for you, Matt," said Rama.

Matt said, "Sam! I did the jump! The bungee did not snap."

Rama ran for the bungee. Matt ran up to Sam.

"You did not fall, Sam," said Rama. "No fall. No snap. I will get the bungee off for you."

"Yes!" said Sam. "I can bungee jump!"

14 *Chapter 1*

What Do You Think?

◆ 1. What sport would you like to try? Why? Check a box, or write your own idea.

❑ sky diving

❑ parasailing

❑ scuba diving

❑ mountain climbing

❑ _____ (your own idea)

2. Write a sentence about a sport you would like to try.

_____

_____

_____

Think About the Story

Use Story Words

◆ **Directions:** Write a word from the box to finish each sentence.

Sam	down	went	Rama

3. The bungee went up and _____.

4. _____ said, "Yes!"

5. _____ ran to Sam.

6. Rama _____ to get the bungee off.

When Did It Happen?

◆ 7. Write a number from 1 to 5 in front of each event to show when it happened.

_____ Rama ran to get the bungee off Matt.

_____ Sam went down, up, down, up, down.

_____ Rama said, "No fall. No snap."

_____ Matt went down, up, down, up, down.

_____ Sam said, "OK, yes. I will jump."

Letters and Sounds

◆ **Directions:** Look at the letter at the beginning of each line. Then say the name of each picture. If the word ends with that letter, write the letter on the line.

t	n

t

1. _____   2. _____   3. _____

n

4. _____   5. _____   6. _____

◆ **Directions:** Say the name of each picture. Circle the letter it ends with.

7.   t   n   8.   t   n   9.   t   n

◆ **Directions:** Write the letters on the lines. See how many words you can make.

m	f	s	t	n	r

10. ca _____   12. ra _____   15. _____ an   18. _____ et

11. ca _____   13. ra _____   16. _____ an   19. _____ et

14. ra _____   17. _____ an   20. _____ et

Story Words

◆ **Directions:** Read each word to yourself. Then say the word out loud. Write the word on the line. Check the box after each step.

is	Read ❑ Say ❑ Write ❑ _____
play	Read ❑ Say ❑ Write ❑ _____
hit	Read ❑ Say ❑ Write ❑ _____
dog	Read ❑ Say ❑ Write ❑ _____
cave	Read ❑ Say ❑ Write ❑ _____
it	Read ❑ Say ❑ Write ❑ _____
ball	Read ❑ Say ❑ Write ❑ _____

◆ **Directions:** Find 2 story words that end with the same letter as the picture. Write the words on the lines.

21. _____   22. _____

More Word Work

TIP: ▶ The letters **a, e, i, o,** and **u** are **vowels.** Sometimes **y** acts as a vowel. The other letters are **consonants.**

◆ **Directions:** Circle each vowel. Draw a line under each consonant.

i   r   a   n   s   o

p   e   b   u   l   m

◆ **Directions:** Unscramble each story word. Write the words on the lines, and circle the vowels.

23. veca   _____

24. hti   _____

25. lalb   _____

1

THE CAVE, PART 1

"Play ball!" said Ann.

Liz said, "I get to hit, OK? Make a play."

Snap! Liz hit the ball. The ball went up. Ann ran to get the ball. Can-Can, the dog, ran to get it. The ball went down. Did Ann get the ball? No. The dog did.

"Can-Can, no!" said Ann. "The ball is not for you."

"You get the ball," said Liz.

"OK, OK. I will," Ann said.

2

Ann said, "I will get a hit." Snap! Ann hit the ball. The ball went up. Liz ran for the ball. Off went Can-Can. The ball went down. Did Liz get the ball? No. Can-Can did.

"Can-Can, no!" said Liz. "Get off the ball! It is not for you!"

3

"Hit the ball, Liz!" said Ann. "I will make a play." Liz hit the ball. Up it went! Can-Can went for it. The ball did not fall down. The dog ran up to a cave.

"A cave!" Ann said. "The ball went down! Can-Can may not get it."

What Do You Think?

◆ 1. Will Can-Can get the ball? Circle your answer.

YES   NO

Think About the Story

Use Story Words

◆ **Directions:** Write a word from the box to finish each sentence.

play	hit	dog	ball	cave

2. Can-Can is a _____.

3. Ann said, "_____ ball!"

4. Liz _____ the ball.

5. Can-Can went for the _____.

6. "A _____!" said Ann.

When Did It Happen?

◆ 7. Write a number from 1 to 4 in front of each event to show when it happened.

_____ Can-Can ran up to a cave.

_____ Ann hit the ball.

_____ The ball did not fall down.

_____ Liz said, "I get to hit, OK?"

Letters and Sounds

◆ **Directions:** Read these words. Circle the vowel in each word.

    1. can   **2.** ran

    3. What vowel did you circle? Write it here. _____

> **TIP:** ▸ The letter **a** can stand for the vowel sound in **can** and **ran**. This vowel sound is the short **a** sound.

◆ **Directions:** Read these words. Circle every word that has the short **a** sound.

4. not	**6.** at	**8.** yes	**10.** snap
5. make	**7.** off	**9.** cave	**11.** man

◆ **Directions:** Write the letters on the lines. See how many words you can make.

    | b | | r | | c | | m | | p | | f |

12. _____ at	**18.** _____ an
13. _____ at	**19.** _____ an
14. _____ at	**20.** _____ an
15. _____ at	**21.** _____ an
16. _____ at	**22.** _____ an
17. _____ at	**23.** _____ an

◆ **Directions:** Write the word that names each picture.

24. _____   **25.** _____

26. _____   **27.** _____

Story Words

Word Bank

Write each of these story words in the Word Bank at the back of this book.

◆ **Directions:** Read each word to yourself. Then say the word out loud. Write the word on the line. Check the box after each step.

we	Read ❑ Say ❑ Write ❑ _____
and	Read ❑ Say ❑ Write ❑ _____
was	Read ❑ Say ❑ Write ❑ _____
of	Read ❑ Say ❑ Write ❑ _____
in	Read ❑ Say ❑ Write ❑ _____
out	Read ❑ Say ❑ Write ❑ _____
need	Read ❑ Say ❑ Write ❑ _____
wall	Read ❑ Say ❑ Write ❑ _____

More Word Work

> **TIP:** The words **bat** and **tan** have a short vowel sound. These words have the consonant-vowel-consonant, or CVC, pattern.

◆ **Directions:** Read these words. Circle the words that have the CVC pattern. Then write the words in the grid.

Example: (pan)   we

28.   no   not

29.   water   mad

30.   nap   need

31.   make   hit

C	V	C
p	a	n

THE CAVE, PART 2

The ball was in the cave. "Rats!" said Ann. "Will Can-Can get the ball?"

"Yes," said Liz. "Get the ball, dog! Get it, Can-Can!" The dog ran in to the cave. A bat went up out of the cave.

"A bat!" said Ann. "Can-Can is in a bat cave! Get out, Can-Can!" The dog ran out of the cave. No ball.

"You get the ball," Ann said.

"You get it!" Liz said.

Ann and Liz went into the bat cave. The ball was up in the wall of the cave.

"You need to jump for it, Ann," said Liz. "We need the ball. Jump up and get it out of the wall."

Ann did jump for the ball. She did not get it. "Jump for it!" Liz said.

"You jump for it," said Ann.

"OK, OK, I will get it," said Liz. Liz went to jump up. "A bat!" she said. A bat went down and out of the cave. The ball went down to Liz.

"We need to get out!" Ann said. Ann and Liz ran out of the bat cave. Can-Can ran out of the cave. A bat went out of the cave. Then Can-Can went for the bat. "No, Can-Can," said Ann. "Do not jump at the bat. We do not need a bat to play ball!"

What Do You Think?

◆ 1. Would you go in a bat cave to get a ball? Circle your answer.
Check a reason, or write your own.

YES	NO
❏ I like bats.	❏ Bats are creepy.
❏ Bats do not scare me.	❏ Bats suck blood.
❏ Bats make good snacks.	❏ Bats can be sick.
❏ _____	❏ _____

2. Write a sentence about bat caves. Tell if you would go in a bat cave, and why or why not.

_____

_____

_____

Think About the Story

Use Story Words

◆ **Directions:** Write a word from the box to finish each sentence.

need	wall	in	out

3. The ball went _____ a cave.

4. The ball was in the _____ of the cave.

5. A bat went _____ of the cave.

6. You _____ a bat to hit a ball.

Why Did It Happen?

◆ **Directions:** Draw a line from each event to the reason it happened.

What Happened	Why
7. Ann and Liz went in the cave.	○ The ball went in the cave.
8. Ann had to jump for the ball.	○ Liz said, "Get the ball, dog!"
9. Can-Can ran in to the cave.	○ The ball was up in the cave wall.

Letters and Sounds

◆ **Directions:** Look at the letter at the beginning of each line. Then say the name of each picture. If the word begins with that letter, write the letter on the line.

| h | l | p |

h

1. _____ 2. _____ 3. _____

l

4. _____ 5. _____ 6. _____

p

7. _____ 8. _____ 9. _____

◆ **Directions:** Write the name of each thing under its picture.

10. _____ 11. _____ 12. _____ 13. _____

Word Bank

Write each of these story words in the Word Bank at the back of this book.

Story Words

◆ **Directions:** Read each word to yourself. Then say the word out loud. Write the word on the line. Check the box after each step.

water (wa | ter)   Read ❑ Say ❑ Write ❑ _____

but   Read ❑ Say ❑ Write ❑ _____

do   Read ❑ Say ❑ Write ❑ _____

like   Read ❑ Say ❑ Write ❑ _____

look   Read ❑ Say ❑ Write ❑ _____

slide   Read ❑ Say ❑ Write ❑ _____

go   Read ❑ Say ❑ Write ❑ _____

◆ **Directions:** Find 2 story words that begin with the same letter as the picture. Write the words on the lines.

14. _____   15. _____

More Word Work

◆ **Directions:** Read these tricky sentences aloud. Practice until you can say each one very fast and get all the words right.

▸ Pat picked a pin and packed it in her pocket.

▸ Lil licked a little mint and put it in her locket.

▸ Hal hid a hammer in a high-flying rocket.

◆ **Directions:** Write 3 words that start with each letter.

h	l	p
16. _____	19. _____	22. _____
17. _____	20. _____	23. _____
18. _____	21. _____	24. _____

AT THE WATER SLIDE, PART 1

Pam, Nan, and Bett went to the water slide. Pam went up the slide, but not down it. Pam sat down on the slide. Pam had a hat on. "Do you like the hat, Bett?" said Pam. "Will Len like it?"

"The hat is OK," said Bett. "And yes, Len will like it. Slide, Pam."

"Go, Pam!" said Nan.

"No," said Pam. "I do not like the water. And I do not like the slide!"

"Pam," said Bett. "Look down the slide. Look at Len, down at the mat."

"Yes, Pam, look at Len," said Nan. "You may not like to slide. You may not like the water. But you like Len. Slide down, Pam. It is a snap. Hit the water and make the hat fall off. Len will get the hat for you. You and the hat will be a hit!"

Pam said, "Yes, I like Len. But I can not go down the slide. I will fall off and hit the water! I will!"

"Look. You need to get Len to fall for you," said Bett. "You can not get Len to look at you if you do not go down the slide. Nan and I will go down. We will get Len in the water, OK? You slide down and make the hat fall. Len will get the hat for you."

What Do You Think?

◆ 1. Is there an easier way to get a person's attention? Circle your answer.

             YES   **NO**

2. What would you do if you wanted to get someone to notice you? Check one answer, or write your own.

   ❑ Trip in front of the person.   ❑ Act funny.

   ❑ Go up and say hi.   ❑ Pretend you need help.

   ❑ _____ (your own idea)

3. Write a sentence telling how you would get someone to notice you.

_____

_____

Think About the Story

Use Story Words

◆ **Directions:** Write a word from the box to finish each sentence.

water	look	slide	go	but

4. Pam went up the _____, but not down it.

5. Pam said, "I do not like the _____."

6. Bett said, "You need to make Len _____ at you."

7. Nan said, "_____, Pam!"

8. Nan and Bett went down the slide, _____ Pam did not.

Why Did It Happen?

◆ **Directions:** Draw a line from each event to the reason it happened.

What Happened	Why
9. Pam did not go down the slide.	○ It will get Len to look at Pam.
10. Bett said, "Make the hat fall off."	○ Len was down on the mat.
11. Nan said, "Look down."	○ Nan and Bett will get Len in the water.
12. Nan and Bett go down the slide.	○ Pam did not like the water.

Letters and Sounds

> **TIP:** ▸ The letter **e** can stand for the vowel sound in **get** and **yes**. This is called the short **e** vowel sound.

◆ **Directions:** Read these words. Circle every word that has the short **e** sound.

1. did   2. can   3. went   4. need   5. let   6. cave

◆ **Directions:** Write the letters on the lines. See how many words you can make.

| p | d | m | s | n | w | h |

7. _____ et   11. _____ en

8. _____ et   12. _____ en

9. _____ et   13. _____ en

10. _____ et   14. _____ en

◆ **Directions:** Read these words. Write each word in the list where it belongs.

snap   ten   hat   sand

net   pat   rent   end

short *a* sound	short *e* sound
15. _____	19. _____
16. _____	20. _____
17. _____	21. _____
18. _____	22. _____

Story Words

Word Bank

Write each of these story words in the Word Bank at the back of this book.

◆ **Directions:** Read each word to yourself. Then say the word out loud. Write the word on the line. Check the box after each step.

way	Read ❑ Say ❑ Write ❑ _____
then	Read ❑ Say ❑ Write ❑ _____
into (in ǀ to)	Read ❑ Say ❑ Write ❑ _____
how	Read ❑ Say ❑ Write ❑ _____
acted (act ǀ ed)	Read ❑ Say ❑ Write ❑ _____
shot	Read ❑ Say ❑ Write ❑ _____

More Word Work

◆ **Directions:** Read the poem. Circle the words that rhyme.

You can bet	Not tall
I like my pet.	Like a wall
Not a cat	Like a pin
Not a rat	This pet is thin.
You can bet	Think hard.
It's not a bat.	Make no mistake.
Not a hen	This pet has to be
Not a wren	a _____.
Not a hog	
Not a dog	

◆ **Directions:** Write the words from the poem that rhyme on the lines.

rhymes with **met**   rhymes with **sat**

23. _____   25. _____

24. _____   26. _____

                             27. _____

AT THE WATER SLIDE, PART 2

Pam said, "Nan and Bett, you slide. No way will I do it."

"Yes you will," said Bett. "Nan and I will slide, then you. 1, 2, 3, get set—Go!"

Bett and Nan went down the slide and shot into the water fall.

Pam said, "OK, I will go. I will make the hat fall into the water. Then Len will get the hat. 1, 2, 3—get set—go!"

Pam went like a jet down the slide. "Look out!" Pam said. Pam hit the water fall and shot into the water cave. Rats! The hat did not fall off.

Then Pam ran into Len!—bam! Len was in the water cave! "Len! How did you…"

Len said, "I like the wet hat, Pam. How did you like the water slide?"

"I did like it!" Pam said. "I went down it like a jet! And I look like a wet cat."

"No," Len said. " I like the wet hat look. But you look like you need to get out of the water."

Len led Pam out of the water cave. Then Pam went out of the water. She ran up to Bett and Nan. "You!" said Pam. "How did you get Len into the water cave?"

"It was a snap," said Bett. "We went into the cave and acted mad. I acted mad at Nan. I acted like I hit Nan. Len went into the water cave to make us get out of the water. Then you went down the slide.

"Way to go, Pam," said Bett. You did not make the hat fall. But you did make Len fall for you!"

What Do You Think?

◆ 1. What is something others think is fun, that you do not want to try or do at all? Check one answer, or write your own.

❑ jump out of an airplane

❑ camp out in the woods

❑ be in a band

❑ raft a wild river

❑ take dance lessons

❑ _____ (your own idea)

2. Write a sentence telling what you do not want to try, and why.

_____

_____

Think About the Story

Use Story Words

◆ **Directions:** Write a word from the box to finish each sentence.

into	shot	way	acted

3. Pam said, "No _____ will I do it."

4. Pam went down the slide and shot _____ the water.

5. Bett _____ mad at Nan.

6. Bett and Nan _____ into the waterfall.

Why Did It Happen?

◆ **Directions:** Draw a line from each event to the reason it happened.

What Happened	Why
7. Pam ran into Len.	○ Bett acted mad at Nan.
8. Len went into the water cave.	○ Pam and her hat got wet.
9. Len said, "I like the wet hat, Pam."	○ Pam shot into the water cave.

Chapter 1: Summary of Skills and Strategies

Let's look back at what you learned in Chapter 1.

Letters and Sounds

◆ You learned . . .

- the letters **a, e, i, o,** and **u** are vowels. Sometimes **y** acts as a vowel. The other letters are consonants.
- the letters **m, f, s, t, n, r, h, l,** and **p** can come at the beginning of a word.
- the letters **n** and **t** can come at the end of a word.
- the letter **a** can stand for the short **a** vowel sound.
- the letter **e** can stand for the short **e** vowel sound.

Stories and Skills

◆ You learned about . . .

- characters who face problems and find solutions.
- characters who bungee jump, play ball, and go down water slides.

◆ You learned . . .

- how to look ahead, or predict, what story characters might do.

Words and Meanings

◆ You learned . . .

- a lot of new words.
- the letter pattern consonant-vowel-consonant, or CVC, usually stands for a short vowel sound.

The chapter review will give you a chance to show what you have learned.

Part A

Summing It Up: Letters and Sounds

> ▸ The letter **a** can stand for the short **a** vowel sound in **cat** and **fan**.
> ▸ The letter **e** can stand for the short **e** vowel sound in **get** and **yes**.

◆ **Directions:** Read these words. Write each word in the list where it belongs.

can	ran	cat	rat
yes	bet	met	set
get	ram		

short *a* sound	short *e* sound
1. _____	6. _____
2. _____	7. _____
3. _____	8. _____
4. _____	9. _____
5. _____	10. _____

◆ **Directions:** Say the name of each picture. Write the letter it begins or ends with on the line.

| n | f | b | p | t | m |

11. _____ an

12. _____ at

13. ca _____

14. ca _____

15. _____ an

16. _____ an

Part B

Summing It Up: More Word Work

> ▸ The letters **a, e, i, o,** and **u** are vowels.
> ▸ Sometimes **y** acts as a vowel.
> ▸ The other letters are consonants.

◆ **Directions:** Read these story words. Circle the vowel in each word.

1. snap	**3.** get	**5.** ball	**7.** was
2. will	**4.** off	**6.** dog	**8.** and

> ▸ The words **tan** and **cat** have a short vowel sound.
> ▸ These words have the consonant-vowel-consonant, or CVC, pattern.

◆ **Directions:** Read each pair of words. Circle the word in each pair that has the CVC pattern. Then write the word in the grid.

	C	V	C

9. need   not

10. can   make

11. off   bat

12. hit   out

13. yes   cave

14. said   did

Part C

Story Words

◆ **Directions:** On the lines below, write the word from the list that matches each clue.

out	up	yes	we
water	fall	off	

1. not "down" _____

2. you and I _____

3. not "in" _____

4. You swim in it. _____

5. not "no" _____

6. not "on" _____

7. go down _____

◆ **Directions:** On the lines below, write a word from the list to finish each sentence.

hit	cave	jump
snap	said	slide
bungee	ball	acted

8. The bungee will not _____.

9. Sam said, "I can not _____."

10. The _____ went up and down and up and down.

11. Ann _____ the ball.

12. A bat was in the _____.

13. Can-Can went for the _____.

14. Pam went down the _____.

15. Len _____, "I like the wet hat, Pam."

16. Bett _____ mad at Nan.

Part D

Who Did What?

◆ **Directions:** This list has the names of the people who were in the stories in Chapter 1. Write a name on the line to finish each sentence.

Sam   Ann   Pam

Matt   Can-Can   Bett

Rama   Len

1. _____ said, "You will not fall."

2. _____ said, "The bungee may snap."

3. _____ got the bungee off for Matt.

4. _____ went into the cave with Ann and Liz.

5. _____ said, "Play ball!"

6. _____ had acted mad at Nan.

7. _____ had a wet hat.

8. _____ led Pam out of the water cave.

◆ **Directions:** Read each sentence. If it is true, write **True** on the line. If it is false, write **False** on the line.

9. Sam can bungee jump. _____

10. Matt said, "I will fall." _____

11. Can-Can went into the cave. _____

12. The cave had bats. _____

13. Liz got the ball from the cave. _____

14. Pam did not fall for Len. _____

15. Nan went down the slide. _____

16. Bett did not get wet. _____

CHAPTER 2

Lesson 1 . . . . page 38
"Paddle and Roll," Part 1

Lesson 2 . . . . page 42
"Paddle and Roll," Part 2

Lesson 3 . . . . page 46
"The Track," Part 1

Lesson 4 . . . . page 50
"The Track," Part 2

Lesson 5 . . . . page 54
"Go Climb a Rock"

Lesson 6 . . . . page 58
"Big Walls!"

Letters and Sounds

◆ **Directions:** Look at the letter at the beginning of each line. Then say the name of each picture. If the word ends with that letter, write the letter on the line.

m	p	n

m

1. _____   2. _____   3. _____

p

4. _____   5. _____   6. _____

n

7. _____   8. _____   9. _____

◆ **Directions:** Write the letters on the lines. See how many words you can make.

v	y	m	r	t	b	c	s	d

10. _____ am   13. _____ ap   17. _____ an

11. _____ am   14. _____ ap   18. _____ an

12. _____ am   15. _____ ap   19. _____ an

              16. _____ ap   20. _____ an

                                  21. _____ an

Story Words

◆ **Directions:** Read each word to yourself. Then say the word out loud. Write the word on the line. Check the box after each step.

kayak (kay | ak)	Read ❑ Say ❑ Write ❑	_____
river (riv | er)	Read ❑ Say ❑ Write ❑	_____
paddle (pad | dle)	Read ❑ Say ❑ Write ❑	_____
roll	Read ❑ Say ❑ Write ❑	_____
learn	Read ❑ Say ❑ Write ❑	_____
this	Read ❑ Say ❑ Write ❑	_____
now	Read ❑ Say ❑ Write ❑	_____
he	Read ❑ Say ❑ Write ❑	_____
with	Read ❑ Say ❑ Write ❑	_____

More Word Work

TIP: ▶ You can add **s** to many words. Add **s** to make a word tell about more than one, or to make it tell about now.

Examples: kayak + s = kayaks

get + s = gets

◆ **Directions:** Add **s** to each word. Write the word, ending, and new word on the lines.

22. make   _____ + _____ = _____

23. jump   _____ + _____ = _____

24. snap   _____ + _____ = _____

25. play   _____ + _____ = _____

26. cave   _____ + _____ = _____

27. need   _____ + _____ = _____

In   180° roll, you need to get out of the kayak.

In a 360° roll, you make the kayak roll down and then up with you in it.

PADDLE AND ROLL, PART 1

"Get in this kayak, Meg," said Jen. "Dan, you get in the tan kayak."

Meg sat down in the kayak. "I am in, man!" Meg said. "Look, Dan—I can tap you with a kayak."

Dan said, "You ram this kayak and I will get you!" Then he sat down in the tan kayak. "OK, I am in. Now, to the river!"

"Not yet," said Jen. "You need to learn how to paddle and how to roll. Then we will go down the river. Now look. This is how you paddle.—1…2…1…2…. We will do kayak laps."

Meg and Dan did as Jen said. The paddles went up and down, up and down, into and out of the water. "I get it," Dan said. "This is a snap." He did get it!

"OK," said Jen. "Now you will learn how to do a 180° roll. Look. This is how you do it." Jen did get the kayak to roll. It went 180°. Jen went down into the water and had to get out of the kayak.

Meg did it. Then Dan did it.

"To make the kayak roll up with you in it, do a 360° roll," Jen said. Jen did a 360° roll. Then Meg and Dan went to do it. Dan did a 180° roll down, but not up. He had to get out of the kayak.

"Rats!" said Dan. "I can roll the kayak down and slide out, but I can not make it roll up. Jen makes it look like a snap."

"You can do it," said Jen.

Dan and Meg got the kayaks to roll down…and up! They did a 360° roll!

"OK," said Jen. "You get it. Now we can hit the river."

What Do You Think?

◆ 1. What do you think will happen when Meg and Dan hit the river? Check a prediction, or write your own.

    ❑ Dan will roll in the kayak.

    ❑ Water will make the kayaks flip.

    ❑ Dan or Meg will get lost.

    ❑ _____ (your own prediction)

2. Write your prediction on the lines.

I think that _____

_____

_____

Think About the Story

Use Story Words

◆ **Directions:** Write a word from the box to finish each sentence.

he	learn	paddle	kayak	river

3. Meg and Dan will _____ how to do a roll.

4. Dan sat down in the tan _____.

5. Dan can roll down, but can _____ roll up?

6. Dan, Meg, and Jen _____ the kayaks down the river.

7. Do not fall into the _____.

When Did It Happen?

◆ 8. Write a number from 1 to 4 in front of each event to show when it happened.

_____ Meg and Dan learn how to paddle.

_____ Meg and Dan did 360° rolls.

_____ Meg and Dan get in the kayaks.

_____ Jen did a 180° roll.

Letters and Sounds

◆ **Directions:** Read these words. Circle the vowel in each word.

1. hit   2. did   3. this

4. What vowel did you circle? Write it here. _____

> **TIP:** ▸ The letter **i** can stand for the vowel sound in **did** and **hit**.
> This is called the short **i** vowel sound.

◆ **Directions:** Read these words. Circle each word that has the short **i** sound.

5. said   7. is   9. slide   11. pit

6. tip   8. like   10. it   12. rid

Two of the words you circled rhyme. Write them here.

13. _____   and   14. _____

◆ **Directions:** Write the letters on the lines. See how many words you can make.

| t | b | w | l | h | f | d |

15. _____ in   19. _____ ip

16. _____ in   20. _____ ip

17. _____ in   21. _____ ip

18. _____ in   22. _____ ip

◆ **Directions:** Unscramble each word. Write the words on the lines, and circle the vowels.

23. n w i   _____

24. e i l k   _____

25. p i d   _____

Word Bank

Write each of these story words in the Word Bank at the back of this book.

Story Words

◆ **Directions:** Read each word to yourself. Then say the word out loud. Write the word on the line. Check the box after each step.

they   Read ❑ Say ❑ Write ❑ _____

rock   Read ❑ Say ❑ Write ❑ _____

were   Read ❑ Say ❑ Write ❑ _____

fast   Read ❑ Say ❑ Write ❑ _____

More Word Work

◆ **Directions:** Read this word: **slide**

26. How many consonants do you see at the beginning of the word?
    _____

27. What consonants are they? _____ and _____

28. How many consonant sounds do you hear at the beginning
    of the word? _____

> **TIP:** Two consonants can come together at the beginning of a word. Blend the two letter sounds together to read the word.

◆ **Directions:** Read each pair of words. Circle each word that begins with a blend.

29. cave	**30.** play	**31.** lip	**32.** trip	**33.** pan
crave	pay	flip	tip	plan

◆ **Directions:** Write a pair of consonants on each line. See how many words you can make.

sw		tr		sl		dr

34. _____ ip   37. _____ im

35. _____ ip   38. _____ im

36. _____ ip   39. _____ im

PADDLE AND ROLL, PART 2

Meg, Dan, and Jen hit the river. They were up for fast water.

Dan said, "I do not need to paddle. Let the river do it. Can I get a nap in now?"

"No naps!" said Jen. "Look at this map, Dan. The river is not fast now. But in a bit, you can bet it will get fast."

"Look at the river!" Meg said with a gasp. They hit the fast water then. The river was like a water slide. The kayaks slid into it like twigs.

"How do we paddle this?" said Dan.

"You will learn fast," said Jen. "Paddle like mad!"

Jen and Meg let the paddles rip! "Look out! Rocks!" Jen said. The water slid down fast and ran off the rocks. Jen and Meg went down the wall of water, but Dan did not make it.

"Look out, Dan!" said Jen. "Ram into the rocks, and you will flip!"

Dan said, "I do not like to hit the rocks. The kayak likes to hit them!" Bam! Dan hit the rocks. The kayak was in a jam. The kayak went up and down as the fast water hit it.

"Get the kayak off the rocks! Ram the rocks with the paddle!" said Jen.

Dan did it. The kayak shot down the rock slide. But then it did a 180° roll. "Dan!" said Meg. Dan was in the kayak. "Dan!"

"Roll up, Dan, roll up!" said Jen. "Flip the kayak up! Do it now, man!"

The kayak did a 180° roll up. Dan was OK.

"Dan, you dog! You did it! You did a 360°!" said Meg.

"Way to go!" said Jen.

"It was not a roll," said Dan with a big grin. "It was a rock and roll!"

You Be the Judge

◆   1. Do you think it is OK to take part in risky sports that could hurt or even kill you? Why or why not? Circle your answer and check a reason. Or write your own reason.

NO	YES
❏ Why risk getting hurt?	❏ Everything is risky in some way.
❏ You could ruin your life.	❏ Danger is exciting.
❏ I'm a chicken.	❏ Taking risks makes you brave.
❏ _____ (your reason)	❏ _____ (your reason)

2. Write your answer on the lines. Be sure to tell why you feel as you do.

_____

_____

Think About the Story

Use Story Words

◆   **Directions:** Write a word from the box to finish each sentence.

fast	they	were	rock

3. The water in the river was _____.

4. The kayak shot down the _____ slide.

5. The kids were up for fast water as _____ hit the river.

6. Big rocks _____ in the river.

When Did It Happen?

◆   7. Write a number from 1 to 5 in front of each event to show when it happened.

_____ Dan did not make it down the wall of water.

_____ The kayak did a 180° roll up.

_____ The kayak did a 180° roll down.

_____ Meg, Dan, and Jen hit the river.

_____ Meg and Jen shot down the water slide.

Letters and Sounds

◆ **Directions:** Look at the letter at the beginning of each line. Then say the name of each picture. If the word begins with that letter, write the letter on the line.

b	d	c

b

1. _____   2. _____   3. _____

d

4. _____   5. _____   6. _____

c

7. _____   8. _____   9. _____

◆ **Directions:** Write the name of each picture on the line.

10. _____   11. _____   12. _____   13. _____

◆ **Directions:** Write the letters on the lines to make 3 new words.

b	d	c

14. _____ rib   15. re _____   16. ca _____

Story Words

◆ **Directions:** Read each word to yourself. Then say the word out loud. Write the word on the line. Check the box after each step.

if   Read ❑ Say ❑ Write ❑ _____

bike   Read ❑ Say ❑ Write ❑ _____

track   Read ❑ Say ❑ Write ❑ _____

think   Read ❑ Say ❑ Write ❑ _____

biggest (big│gest) Read ❑ Say ❑ Write ❑ _____

his   Read ❑ Say ❑ Write ❑ _____

us   Read ❑ Say ❑ Write ❑ _____

had   Read ❑ Say ❑ Write ❑ _____

dirt   Read ❑ Say ❑ Write ❑ _____

More Word Work

◆ **Directions:** Read this tricky rhyme aloud. Practice until you can say it fast and get all the words right.

> Betty Botter bought some butter.
> "But," she said, "this butter's bitter.
> If I put it in my batter,
> It will make my batter bitter."
> So Betty Botter bought some butter
> Better than the bitter butter
> To make her bitter batter better.

◆ **Directions:** Make up your own tongue twister using the letter **d.** Start with this line:

17. Did Danny Docker dunk a donut?

_____

_____

_____

18. What consonant is repeated the most in the rhyme? Write it here. _____

THE TRACK, PART 1

"This jump is bad," said Daniel. "Now hit the lip, Benny!"

Benny ran his dirt bike up to the lip of the jump. The bike hit the dirt lip and went off the jump. It went down fast and hit the dirt.

"I like this jump," said Benny. "We can set up laps, Daniel. I think we can make this dirt pit into the biggest bike track," he said. "We can dig out dips. We can make a pit to jump."

Bap! A bike ran into Daniel. It was Tim, on his dirt bike. He had a mad look.

Bam! A bike ran into Benny. It was Cameron. He had a mad look. "Bam!" said Cameron. "How do you like this, Tim? They think they can jump."

"Get off this track, you dips!" said Tim.

"Yes, get off!" said Cameron.

"No way!" said Benny. "You can not make us get off this track!"

"Dips?" said Daniel. "We do not look like dips! We make dips…and jumps…. And I bet we can out-jump you. We can jump you off this track!"

"Get this, Cam!" said Tim. "The kid thinks he can jump us off the track."

"They can not do it," said Cameron. "You and I make the biggest jumps!"

"OK, then," said Benny. "We make 3 laps. Then you make 3 laps. If you make the biggest jump, then you get the track. If you fall, you get out. And if we make the biggest jumps, and we do not fall, then we get the track. OK?"

You Be the Judge

◆ 1. Do you think Benny's idea is a good one? Circle your answer.

   YES   NO

2. What would you have done when Cameron and Tim showed up?

_____

_____

Think About the Story

Use Story Words

◆ **Directions:** Write a word from the box to finish each sentence.

had	bike	dirt	biggest	track

3. Benny is on a dirt _____.

4. Daniel said, "We can jump you off this _____!"

5. Cameron thinks he and Tim can make the _____ jumps.

6. Tim and Cameron _____ mad looks.

7. Benny's bike hit the _____.

When Did It Happen?

◆ 8. Write a number from 1 to 4 in front of each event to show when it happened.

_____ Benny said, "If you make the biggest jump, then you get the track."

_____ Benny thinks they can dig out dips.

_____ Daniel said, "I bet we can out-jump you."

_____ Tim ran his bike into Daniel.

Letters and Sounds

◆ **Directions:** Look at the letter at the beginning of each line. Then say the name of each picture. If the word begins with that letter, write the letter on the line.

| k | v | j |

k

1. _____   2. _____   3. _____

v

4. _____   5. _____   6. _____

j

7. _____   8. _____   9. _____

◆ **Directions:** Write the letters on the lines. See how many words you can make.

| k | v | j |

10. _____ am   11. _____ et   13. _____id   14. _____ob

12. _____et

Story Words

◆ **Directions:** Read each word to yourself. Then say the word out loud. Write the word on the line. Check the box after each step.

all	Read ❏ Say ❏ Write ❏ _____
made	Read ❏ Say ❏ Write ❏ _____
bump	Read ❏ Say ❏ Write ❏ _____
very (ver | y)	Read ❏ Say ❏ Write ❏ _____
keep	Read ❏ Say ❏ Write ❏ _____
that	Read ❏ Say ❏ Write ❏ _____

More Word Work

◆ **Directions:** Write each story word inside the shape that fits it. One has been done for you.

15.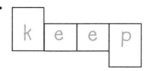

16.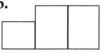

17.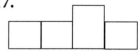

18.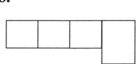

19.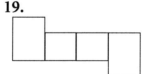

20.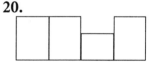

◆ **Directions:** Write the letters or letter pairs on the lines. See how many words you can make.

f	b	w	c	sm	t

21. _____ all   **24.** _____ all

22. _____ all   **25.** _____ all

23. _____ all   **26.** _____ all

THE TRACK, PART 2

"Let the dips make 3 laps," said Cameron. "They can not out-jump us!"

"OK!" said Benny. "Jam it, Daniel!" Daniel made his bike go very fast. Dirt shot up in back of his bike. Benny went all out. Lap 1. The bikes sped like jets on the track. They hit the bumps like bats out of a cave. Lap 2!

"Yes, Benny! Go, man!" said Daniel. "Keep it up!" They sped out of lap 3.

"OK, big shots. Now you go," Benny said to Tim.

Tim and Cameron hit the track very fast. They made all the biggest jumps and bumps. They made 3 laps look like a snap. Cameron was fast—very fast.

"They can do all the big jumps," said Benny. "And man, can they go!"

"Tim acts like a big shot," Daniel said. "But he is OK. And yes, they can jam on bikes."

Cameron and Tim made a last big jump. The bikes hit the dirt in a skid that sent rocks up. "How about that?" Cameron said with a big grin.

"Not bad," said Benny. "Not bad at all. But no way did you make the biggest jump. Now we all do a lap. The kids that make it back to that rock fastest will win it all. OK?"

"You got it!" Tim shot back, and the bikes were off. They went like mad up and down the bumps. Then they made a roll to make the biggest jump of all. Up, up, up they went, and then down! Tim and Benny hit bikes on the way down. Then Cameron and Daniel hit. "Look out!" Tim said. Bam! Bam! Bam! Bam!

Benny, Cameron, Tim, and Daniel all sat in the dirt. "This is bad," said Tim. "We do not get the track. And you do not get it."

"How is it if we all keep the track?" said Daniel. And they did.

What Do You Think?

◆ 1. If you found a place for fun like the kids in this story, what would you do with it? Draw a picture of how you would set it up.

Think About the Story

Use Story Words

◆ **Directions:** Write a word from the box to finish each sentence.

bump	all	very	keep

2. _____ the kids made big jumps.

3. Daniel said, "_____ it up !"

4. The dirt bike hit a _____.

5. The bikes went _____ fast!

What Are the Facts?

◆ **Directions:** Write **True** next to the sentences that are true. Write **False** next to the sentences that are false.

6. _____ The kids made 4 laps.

7. _____ Cameron was very fast.

8. _____ Tim and Cameron got to keep the track.

9. _____ The kids all made big jumps.

Letters and Sounds

◆ **Directions:** Read these words. Circle the consonants at the end of each word.

1. track   2. roll

3. How many consonants did you circle at the end of each word? _____

4. How many consonant sounds do you hear at the end of **track,** 1 or 2? _____

5. How many consonant sounds do you hear at the end of **roll,** 1 or 2? _____

> **TIPS:** ▸ When the letters **ck** come at the end of a word, they stand for one sound—the **k** sound.
>
> ▸ When the letters **ll** come a the end of a word they stand for one sound—the **l** sound.

◆ **Directions:** Read these words. Draw a line under 3 words that end with the **l** sound in **roll.** Circle 3 words that end with the **k** sound in **track.**

6. bell   8. act   10. wall   12. stack

7. pick   9. will   11. rock   13. melt

◆ **Directions:** Write each word you marked next to the word it rhymes with.

14. rack _____   16. pill _____   18. sell _____

15. sick _____   17. sock _____   19. tall _____

◆ **Directions:** Write the letters on the lines. See how many words you can make.

t	w	s	p	b	m	f	sm

20. _____ill   26. _____ell

21. _____ill   27. _____ell

22. _____ill   28. _____ell

23. _____ill   29. _____ell

24. _____ill   30. _____ell

25. _____ill   31. _____ell

Story Words

Word Bank

Write each of these story words in the Word Bank at the back of this book.

◆ **Directions:** Read each word to yourself. Then say the word out loud. Write the word on the line. Check the box after each step.

slow   Read ❑ Say ❑ Write ❑ _____

climb   Read ❑ Say ❑ Write ❑ _____

from   Read ❑ Say ❑ Write ❑ _____

she   Read ❑ Say ❑ Write ❑ _____

about (a│bout)   Read ❑ Say ❑ Write ❑ _____

rope   Read ❑ Say ❑ Write ❑ _____

carabiner   Read ❑ Say ❑ Write ❑ _____

(car│a│bi│ner)

belay (be│lay)   Read ❑ Say ❑ Write ❑ _____

More Word Work

TIP: ▸ You can add **ed** to many verbs. Do this to make the verb tell about the past.

Now: I **lock** up the bikes.   **The Past:** I **locked** up the bikes.

◆ **Directions:** Write the sentences below again. Make each one tell about the past. To do this, add **ed** to the **bold** word.

Example: The kids **act** mad at Tim.
            The kids acted mad at Tim.

32. Tim and Dan **jump** on the bikes.

_____

33. We **pick** the biggest kayak.

_____

34. "I **smell** a rat," said Rick.

_____

1 GO CLIMB A ROCK

Look up. It is a wall of rock. Up and up and up you look. Can you get up that rock? No way. But Jill and Nell did. This is about how they did it.

A rope led from Jill, up to the rim, and back down to Nell. Jill had to get a pin and a carabiner out of a pack. She tacked the pin and carabiner into the rock. She had to tap it in well. The pin has to go into the rock and stick! Then she fed the rope into the carabiner.

2

You may ask, "How do the rope, the carabiners, and the pins help in a climb like this?" Well, if Jill falls, the rope hits the pin and slows the fall. Jill will not fall off the rock and go down, down, down…well, you get it.

Nell had the rope. She said, "OK, I will belay you, Jill. Go on! Climb up!" As Jill climbed up, Nell let the rope out bit by bit. You may ask, "What can Nell do if Jill falls?" If Jill falls now, Nell needs to let out the rope as slow as she can.

3

Jill climbed up and up. She was about to get to the very rim of the rock. At last, she was on the rim. But what about Nell? How did she get up to the rim?

Now Jill had the rope. The rope went from the rim down to Nell. "OK, belay me!" Nell said. Nell climbed to the pin in the rock. She picked the pin and carabiner out of the rock. They went into her pack. Then Nell climbed up to the rim.

Now. Can you get up that rock? Bet you can.

LESSON 5 — After Reading "Go Climb a Rock"

What Do You Think?

◆ 1. Would you like to try to climb a rock? Circle your answer. Check a reason, or write your own.

YES	NO
❑ I like to climb things.	❑ It looks too scary.
❑ Rock climbing looks fun.	❑ It looks like work, not play.
❑ I like thrills.	❑ Do I look like a mountain goat?
❑ _____	❑ _____
(your reason)	(your reason)

2. Write your answer. Tell why you would or would not like to try rock climbing.

_____

_____

Think About the Story

Use Story Words

◆ **Directions:** Write a word from the box to finish each sentence.

slow	she	climb	carabiner	rope

3. To _____ a rock is to go up to the top.

4. You need a _____ to belay a pal up a rock.

5. The rope needs to go into the _____.

6. Did Jill climb fast or _____?

7. _____ made it up to the top!

When Did It Happen?

◆ 8. Write a number from 1 to 4 in front of each event to show when it happened.

_____ Jill climbed up the rock.

_____ Nell made it to the top of the rock.

_____ Jill belayed Nell.

_____ Jill tacked the pin and carabiner into the rock.

Lesson 5 **57**

Letters and Sounds

◆ **Directions:** Read these words. Circle the vowel in each word.

1. rock

2. shot

3. What vowel did you circle? Write it here. _____

> **TIP:** ▸ The letter **o** can stand for the vowel sound in **rock** and **shot**. This vowel sound is the short **o** sound.

◆ **Directions:** Read these words. Circle every word that has the short **o** sound.

4. no	6. you	8. not	10. pond
5. rope	7. stop	9. mock	11. lock

◆ **Directions:** Write the letters on the lines. See how many words you can make.

l	d	m	r	p	h	dr	cl

12. _____ ock	17. _____ op	21. _____ ack
13. _____ ock	18. _____ op	22. _____ ack
14. _____ ock	19. _____ op	23. _____ ack
15. _____ ock	20. _____ op	24. _____ ack
16. _____ ock		

◆ **Directions:** Circle 6 words that have a short vowel sound. Write each word in the chart where it belongs.

25. play	27. then	29. pop	31. tell
26. pan	28. need	30. dock	32. lack

short *a*	short *o*	short *e*
33. _____	35. _____	37. _____
34. _____	36. _____	38. _____

Story Words

Directions: Read each word to yourself. Then say the word out loud. Write the word on the line. Check the box after each step.

world   Read ❑ Say ❑ Write ❑ _____

where   Read ❑ Say ❑ Write ❑ _____

challenge (chal|lenge) Read ❑ Say ❑ Write ❑ _____

these   Read ❑ Say ❑ Write ❑ _____

vertical (ver|ti|cal)   Read ❑ Say ❑ Write ❑ _____

what   Read ❑ Say ❑ Write ❑ _____

face   Read ❑ Say ❑ Write ❑ _____

over (o|ver)   Read ❑ Say ❑ Write ❑ _____

feet   Read ❑ Say ❑ Write ❑ _____

are   Read ❑ Say ❑ Write ❑ _____

More Word Work

> **TIP:** ▶ You can add **ing** to many verbs. Do this to make a verb tell about something that is happening now.
>
> **The past:** I **climbed** to the top.   **Now:** I am **climbing** to the top.

39. What word was added to the sentence that tells about now?

_____

Directions: Add **ing** to each word. Then write the word in the sentence.

Example: look → looking   Nell is looking at the rock.

40. slow   → _____ That kid is _____ me down.

41. bump → _____ Jan keeps _____ into me!

Directions: You know that adding **ed** to a verb makes it tell about the past. Write these sentences again. Make each verb tell about the past.

42. I water the plants. _____

43. Nell learns to kayak. _____

BIG WALLS

Got carabiners? Got a rope? Got a climbing pal? OK! Now you are set to go vertical. But you need facts about where to go and what to climb. These are about the biggest climbing walls in the world. You can bet that these walls are a BIG challenge!

These are the Trango Towers in Pakistan. They are the biggest vertical faces in the world. These rocks are over 4,000 feet tall! What a climb!

Do not look down! This wall in India has a face that is 3,500 feet tall. If you fall from a rock like this, it is all over.

This is Troll Wall in Norway. It has a vertical face of 3,300 feet. This big wall challenges the best of the best. No bungee jumping from this spot!

Look at Mt. Asgard. It is in Canada, in the Canadian Arctic. It is over 3,000 feet tall. Now that is a big rock! How do you get to the top? You learn how to climb very, very well!

What Do You Think?

◆ 1. You may not get to Pakistan or Norway. But you may have a climbing wall in your town. Why are climbing walls so popular? Write your answer on the lines.

_____

_____

Think About the Story

Use Story Words

◆ **Directions:** Write a word from the box to finish each sentence.

world	over	challenge	vertical	where

2. These walls are a big _____ to climb.

3. Mt. Asgard is _____ 3,000 feet tall!

4. Troll Wall has a _____ face of 3,300 feet.

5. There are big rocks all over the _____.

6. _____ are the Trango Towers?

What's the Big Idea?

◆ 7. Circle the sentence that tells what "Big Walls!" is mostly about.

    a. "Big Walls!" is about a vertical rock wall in Norway.

    b. "Big Walls!" is about some of the biggest climbing walls in the world.

    c. "Big Walls!" is about how to climb big rocks.

How Tall Are They?

◆ 8. Make a graph showing how tall the 4 vertical walls in this story are. Use the graph on the left as a model.

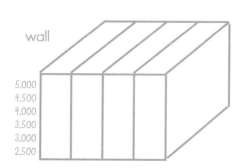

Chapter 2: Summary of Skills and Strategies

Let's look back at what you learned in Chapter 2.

Letters and Sounds

◆ You learned . . .

- ‣ more letters that can come at the beginning or end of words.
- ‣ sometimes two consonants at the end of a word can stand for one sound.
- ‣ the letter **i** can stand for the short **i** vowel sound.
- ‣ the letter **o** can stand for the short **o** vowel sound.

Stories and Skills

◆ You learned about . . .

- ‣ characters who kayak, ride dirt bikes, and go rock climbing.
- ‣ some of the biggest rock walls in the world.

◆ You learned . . .

- ‣ how to look ahead, or predict, what story characters might do.

Words and Meanings

◆ You learned . . .

- ‣ a lot of new words.
- ‣ sometimes when two consonants come at the beginning of a word, you can blend the two letter sounds together.
- ‣ you can add **s** to many words to tell about more than one, or to tell about something that is happening now.
- ‣ you can add **ed** to many verbs to tell about the past.
- ‣ you can add **ing** to many verbs to tell about something happening now.

The chapter review will give you a chance to show what you have learned.

Part A

Summing It Up: Letters and Sounds

> ▶ The letter **i** can stand for the short **i** vowel sound in **hit**.
> ▶ The letter **o** can stand for the short **o** vowel sound in **shot**.

◆ **Directions:** Read these words. Write each word in the list where it belongs.

dock	stop	tip	mop
tin	is	lock	this

short *i*	short *o*
1. _____	5. _____
2. _____	6. _____
3. _____	7. _____
4. _____	8. _____

◆ **Directions:** Say the name of each picture. Write the letter it begins or ends with on the line.

| c | m | k | p | b | v | n | j | d |

9. _____ at   10. _____ ey   11. ca _____

12. ma _____   13. da _____   14. _____ an

15. _____ ake   16. _____ am   17. _____ og

Part B

Summing It Up: More Word Work

> ▸ Two consonants can come together at the beginning of a word. Blend the two letter sounds together to read the word.

◆ **Directions:** Read each pair of words. Circle each word that begins with a blend.

1. top	2. sip	3. blend	4. snap	5. play	6. pin
stop	skip	bend	nap	pay	spin

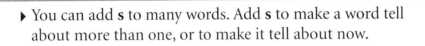
> ▸ You can add **s** to many words. Add **s** to make a word tell about more than one, or to make it tell about now.

◆ **Directions:** Add **s** to each word. Write the word, **s,** and the new word on the lines.

7. play _____ + _____ = _____

8. rope _____ + _____ = _____

9. keep _____ + _____ = _____

10. track _____ + _____ = _____

> ▸ You can add **ed** to many verbs. Do this to make the verb tell about the past.

◆ **Directions:** Write the sentences below again. Make each one tell about the past. To do this, add **ed** to the **bold** word.

11. Steve and Abby **roll** down a hill.

_____

12. They **bump** into a wall.

_____

13. The kids **need** pads!

_____

▶ You can add **ing** to many verbs. Do this to make a verb tell about something that is happening now.

◆ **Directions:** Add **ing** to each word. Then write the word in the sentence.

14. go _____ Bill is _____ to the water slide.

15. think _____ Pam is _____ of a plan.

16. climb _____ Now she is _____ the wall.

Part C

Story Words

◆ **Directions:** On the lines below, write the word from the list that matches each clue.

run	climb	river	bump	slow	they

1. not fast _____

2. he and she _____

3. go fast with feet _____

4. go up _____

5. water that keeps going _____

6. fall on a rock and get this _____

◆ **Directions:** On the lines below, write a word from the list to finish each sentence.

made	bike	paddle	kayak
carabiner	rock	keep	

7. To go in a kayak, you _____.

8. A _____ in a river can make a kayak flip.

9. Dan did a 180° roll in a _____.

10. Benny went off a jump with his dirt _____.

11. Tim and Cameron _____ big jumps with bikes.

12. To climb a big wall, you will need a _____.

13. Rope and carabiners can _____ you from falling off a rock.

Part D

Think About the Stories

Who Did What?

◆ **Directions:** This list has the names of the people who were in the stories in Chapter 2. Write a name on the line to finish each sentence.

Tim   Nell   Jill

Jen   Dan   Benny

1. _____ said, "I did a rock and roll."

2. _____ made a 360° roll look like a snap.

3. _____ said, "I think we can make this dirt pit into the biggest bike track."

4. _____ had a mad look on his face, and he ran into Daniel.

5. _____ picked the pin and the carabiner out of the rock.

6. _____ got to the rim and then belayed her pal.

◆ **Directions:** Read each sentence. If it is true, write **True** on the line. If it is false, write **False** on the line.

7. _____ You paddle a kayak 1…2…3…1…2…3…

8. _____ Jen and Meg did not flip the kayaks.

9. _____ Tim called Benny and Daniel dips.

10. _____ Tim and Cameron made the biggest jumps and got the track.

11. _____ Benny and Daniel made it back to the rock fastest and got the track.

12. _____ Jill and Nell did not fall off the rock.

13. _____ Jill made it to the top, but Nell did not.

14. _____ The biggest vertical faces in the world are in the United States.

15. _____ The Trango Towers in Pakistan are over 4,000 feet tall.

CHAPTER 3

Lesson 1 . . . . page 68
   "Kick-It-Back"

Lesson 2 . . . . page 72
   "The Sub Comes Up"

Lesson 3 . . . . page 76
   "Airplane Quiz"

Lesson 4 . . . . page 80
   "Night Jump!"

Lesson 5 . . . . page 84
   "Karate"

Lesson 6 . . . . page 88
   "Karate Cool"

Letters and Sounds

◆ **Directions:** Look at the letter at the beginning of each line. Then say the name of each picture. If the word begins with that letter, write the letter on the line.

w	g	z

w

 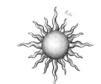

1. _____   2. _____   3. _____

g

4. _____   5. _____   6. _____

z

7. _____   8. _____   9. _____

> **TIP:** ▶ The letters **wh** come together at the beginning of some words.
> **Wh** can have the **h** sound in **who**. **Wh** can have the **w** sound in **when**.

◆ **Directions:** Write the letters on the lines. See how many words you can make.

w	wh	g	z

10. _____ ip   12. _____ et   14. _____ en

11. _____ ip   13. _____ et

◆ **Directions:** Find 4 words that begin with **w** or **wh.** Circle the words and write them on the lines.

w	i	n	x	w	p
h	x	t	i	o	n
a	w	h	e	r	e
t	y	o	t	k	k

15. _____

16. _____

17. _____

18. _____

Word Bank

Write each of these story words in the Word Bank at the back of this book.

Story Words

◆ **Directions:** Read each word to yourself. Then say the word out loud. Write the word on the line. Check the box after each step.

time	Read ❑ Say ❑ Write ❑ _____
come	Read ❑ Say ❑ Write ❑ _____
your	Read ❑ Say ❑ Write ❑ _____
my	Read ❑ Say ❑ Write ❑ _____
again (a | gain)	Read ❑ Say ❑ Write ❑ _____

More Word Work

Let's sum up what you know about words and endings.

> ‣ You can add **s** to many words to make them tell about more than one.
>
> ‣ You can add **ed** to many verbs to make them tell about the past.
>
> ‣ You can add **ing** to many verbs to make them tell about now.

◆ **Directions:** Add an ending to each word. Write the new word on the line.

Examples: challenge + s   = challenges

    belay + ed   = belayed

    climb + ing   = climbing

19. world + s   = _____

20. track + ing   = _____

21. bump + ed   = _____

22. kayak + s   = _____

◆ **Directions:** Read these words. Then write the word and the ending.

Example: kayaking = kayak + ing

23. thinking   = _____ + _____

24. jumped   = _____ + _____

25. watered   = _____ + _____

26. paddles   = _____ + _____

KICK-IT-BACK

Willis sat on the deck. It was hot out—very hot. Willis had a lot of time on his hands. "What can I do?" he said. "Playing ball is not OK when it is this hot. I do not like the water. My bike is shot. What can I do?"

Whap! A sack went over the deck wall and fell on the deck. Willis picked up the bag. It was red. It was not big at all. It was filled with small rocks.

"What is this bag?" said Willis. "Where did it come from? How did it get up on my deck?" Willis went over to the deck wall. He looked up. He looked down. A kid, Zack, looked up at him.

"Did a ball fall on your deck?" said Zack.

"This bag is a ball?" said Willis.

"Come on! Kick it back!" said Zack.

"You kick it?" Willis kicked the sack. *Whap! Zip!* It shot up and over the deck wall. "Looks like you get your bag back," he said to Zack.

But the sack did not fall. Zack kicked it up. It fell and he kicked it up again. *Whap! Whap!* He kicked it up again and again. *Whap! Zip!* The bag shot back up and fell on the deck with a small pop.

Willis picked it up and kicked it back to Zack. *Whap!*

Whap! Zip! Whop! Zap! The bag went fast over the wall, down to Zack, and then back up.

"This is OK!" said Willis. "I like kicking this bag! I like this kick-it-back! Zack, can I learn from you? I will come down in a bit. We can kick your kick-it-back!"

What Do You Think?

◆ 1. Why is kick-it-back a good game for Willis? Write your answer. Use words from the story.

_____

_____

_____

Think About the Story

Use Story Words

◆ **Directions:** Write a word from the box to finish each sentence.

come	your	again	time

2. Can I look at _____ sack?

3. Zack kicked the sack. Then he kicked it _____.

4. What _____ is it?

5. Can you _____ over to play ball?

When Did It Happen?

◆ 6. Write a number from 1 to 4 in front of each event to show when it happened.

_____ Zack looks for his sack.

_____ Willis picks up a small red bag.

_____ Willis asks Zack if he can learn from him.

_____ Willis and Zack kick the sack up and back.

Why Did It Happen?

◆ **Directions:** Draw a line from each event to the reason it happened.

What Happened	Why
7. Willis said, "It looks like you get your bag back."	○ A red sack fell on the deck.
8. "What is this?" said Willis.	○ He likes kicking the sack.
9. "I will come down in a bit," Willis said.	○ Willis kicked the sack down to Zack.

Letters and Sounds

◆ **Directions:** Read these words. Circle the vowel in each word.

1. up   2. bump   3. us

4. What vowel did you circle? Write it here. _____

> **TIP:** ▸ The letter **u** can stand for the vowel sound in **bump** and **us**. This is called the short **u** sound.

◆ **Directions:** Circle each word that has a short **u** sound in it.

5. luck   7. you   9. rut
6. jump   8. out   10. fun

◆ **Directions:** Write the letters on the lines. See how many words you can make.

b	d	g	h	l	p	t	y

11. _____ um   15. _____ uck   19. _____ ug

12. _____ um   16. _____ uck   20. _____ ug

13. _____ um   17. _____ uck   21. _____ ug

14. _____ um   18. _____ uck   22. _____ ug

◆ **Directions:** Read these words. Write each word in the chart where it belongs.

shot   picked   pump   flick   tops
jump   socked   bins   runs   drums

short *i* sound	short *o* sound	short *u* sound
23. _____	26. _____	29. _____
24. _____	27. _____	30. _____
25. _____	28. _____	31. _____
		32. _____

Story Words

Word Bank

Write each of these story words in the Word Bank at the back of this book.

◆ **Directions:** Read each word to yourself. Then say the word out loud. Write the word on the line. Check the box after each step.

first	Read ❑ Say ❑ Write ❑ _____
could	Read ❑ Say ❑ Write ❑ _____
see	Read ❑ Say ❑ Write ❑ _____
find	Read ❑ Say ❑ Write ❑ _____
torpedo (tor⎪pe⎪do)	Read ❑ Say ❑ Write ❑ _____
year	Read ❑ Say ❑ Write ❑ _____
ship	Read ❑ Say ❑ Write ❑ _____
one	Read ❑ Say ❑ Write ❑ _____

More Word Work

◆ **Directions:** Add an ending from the box to each word to make a word that fits in the sentence. Write the new word on the line.

ed	ing	s

Example: your   This is my paddle, and that one is yours.

33. climb   That kid is _____ up the rock!

34. look   I _____ at the map with Val.

35. dog   I think _____ make the best pets.

36. bump   There are a lot of _____ on the track.

37. play   Kids like _____ in the mud.

38. roll   The balls _____ into the water and got lost.

39. track   I _____ you down at last.

40. learn   Nat is _____ to paddle a kayak.

THE SUB COMES UP

It was February 17, 1864. The Confederate Navy sub, *H.L. Hunley*, went out to the waters off Charleston, South Carolina. It snuck up on the *U.S.S. Housatonic*, a big U.S. Navy ship. The 150 men on the ship *Housatonic* were in for it. The sub let a torpedo go. The torpedo was held back by a big rope. With a snap of the rope, the torpedo was set off. It hit the *Housatonic* with a whack! The torpedo went off. Bam! The men on the *Housatonic* could not tell what had hit the ship. The *Housatonic* went down fast. This was a big win for the Confederate Navy! The *Hunley* was the first sub in the world to torpedo a ship and send it down.

The *Hunley* was not hit. It was on its way back to Charleston, but it did not make it. The *Hunley* went down. No one learned just how it went down. And no one could find it for over 130 years. Then, in 1995, a find was made. The *Hunley* was where it went down in 1864. It sat in the mud in the water off Charleston. In the year 2000, a ship went to the spot where the *Hunley* was. It got the *Hunley* out of the mud and back up on top of the water. The hull of the sub had mud all over it. For the first time in 136 years, the *Hunley* could go back to Charleston.

But you can not get a look at the *Hunley* yet. First it has to be dug out of all the mud stuck to it. That job is a big one! Then the *Hunley* has to sit in a big tub of water for 7 years to keep out rot. In about ten years, the *Hunley* could be a fun sub for *you* to find!

You Be the Judge

1. Do you think people should spend time and money looking for things from the past, such as the *Hunley*? Why or why not? Circle an answer and check a reason. Or, write your own reason.

<table>
<tr><td align="center">**YES**</td><td align="center">**NO**</td></tr>
<tr><td>❏ History is important.</td><td>❏ Other things are more important.</td></tr>
<tr><td>❏ We can learn from the past.</td><td>❏ The past is over, so let it go.</td></tr>
<tr><td>❏ _____
(your reason)</td><td>❏ _____
(your reason)</td></tr>
</table>

2. Now write your answer.

_____

_____

Think About the Story

Use Story Words

Directions: Write a word from the box that fits each clue.

torpedo	ship	first	find	one	see

3. to look   _____

4. can hit with a big whack   _____

5. not last   _____

6. 1   _____

7. to get what was lost   _____

8. can sit on top of the water   _____

What Are the Facts?

Directions: Write **True** next to the sentences that are true. Write **False** next to the sentences that are false.

9. _____ In the year 2000, the *U.S.S. Housatonic* was dug out.

10. _____ In 1864, the *Hunley* hit the *Housatonic* with a torpedo.

11. _____ No one learned how the *Hunley* went down.

12. _____ The *Hunley* is still down in the water and mud off Charleston.

Letters and Sounds

> **TIPS:**
> ▸ The letters **qu** come together at the beginning of many words. The letters **qu** stand for the **kw** sound you hear in **quick**.
>
> ▸ The letter **x** comes at the end of some words. It stands for the **ks** sound you hear at the end of **mix**.

◆ **Directions:** Read these words. Circle the words that begin with the **kw** sound in **quick.**

1. quiz   2. camp   3. quack   4. quit

◆ **Directions:** Read these words. Circle the words that end with the sound you hear in **mix.**

5. fix   6. face   7. licks   8. tux

◆ **Directions:** Find the word from the box that fits each clue. Write the word on the line.

quick	wax	six	quit
fix	quiz	quack	ax

9. to mend _____

10. what a duck can do _____

11. fast _____

12. what you cut logs with _____

13. a test _____

14. 6 _____

15. can drip _____

16. to stop _____

◆ **Directions:** Draw a line from each word on the left to the word on the right it rhymes with.

17. quit   stack

18. mix   fax

19. quack   picks

20. wax   fit

Story Words

Word Bank

Write each of these story words in the Word Bank at the back of this book.

◆ **Directions:** Read each word to yourself. Then say the word out loud. Write the word on the line. Check the box after each step.

airplane (air | plane)   Read ❑ Say ❑ Write ❑ _____

exit (ex | it)   Read ❑ Say ❑ Write ❑ _____

mask   Read ❑ Say ❑ Write ❑ _____

seat belt   Read ❑ Say ❑ Write ❑ _____

under (un | der)   Read ❑ Say ❑ Write ❑ _____

check   Read ❑ Say ❑ Write ❑ _____

be   Read ❑ Say ❑ Write ❑ _____

More Word Work

◆ **Directions:** Find a word from the box to finish each rhyme. Write the words on the lines.

quack	tux	quit	sub

21. I need big bucks
    To get a _____.

22. In my tub
    I keep a _____.

23. If the ducks come back,
    Give me a _____.

24. I will have a fit
    If you _____.

> **TIP:** Some words are made up of two smaller words.
>
> **Example:** caveman = cave + man

◆ **Directions:** Read these words. Write the two smaller words that make up each word.

25. airplane = _____ + _____

26. doghouse = _____ + _____

AIRPLANE QUIZ

Going on an airplane trip? You need to be up on these airplane tips. This quiz will let you check out your "airplane I.Q."

A. Directions: Pick the answer that finishes each sentence. Circle the correct answer.

1. Your _____ bags need to be checked.
   a. best
   b. red
   c. biggest
   d. wet

2. A bag needs to fit in the _____ over your seat.
   a. can
   b. pan
   c. pot
   d. bin

3. One bag can be down under the _____, as well.
   a. well
   b. ship
   c. seat
   d. rug

4. Keep your seat belt _____.
   a. on at all times
   b. on if seated
   c. in the bin
   d. filled with water

5. If you need air, a _____ will fall for you.
   a. seat belt
   b. paddle
   c. torpedo
   d. mask

6. If your plane is going to go _____, look for an exit quick.
   a. down
   b. fast
   c. up
   d. kayaking

B. Directions: Look at this airplane. Then follow the directions.

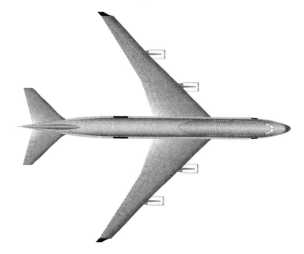

7. Make an **X** by the exits.

What Do You Think?

◆ 1. What is the best way to travel? Why? Check an answer and a reason, or write your own answer.

Best Way to Travel
- ❏ car
- ❏ bike
- ❏ airplane
- ❏ _____ (your own idea)

Reason
- ❏ fast
- ❏ fun
- ❏ cheap
- ❏ _____ (your own reason)

2. Write a sentence about the best way to travel. Tell why you think it is the best.

_____

_____

Think About the Story

Use Story Words

◆ **Directions:** Write a word from the box to solve each clue.

under	exit	mask	airplane	seat belt

3. You put this on if you need air. _____

4. Look for this if you need to get off the plane.

_____

5. You must put this on in an airplane. _____

6. If it is not over, it can be _____.

7. You get on this to go on a big trip. _____

What Are the Facts?

◆ **Directions:** Write **True** next to each sentence that is true. Write **False** next to each sentence that is false.

8. _____ You do not need a seat belt on an airplane.

9. _____ You can not bring bags on a plane.

10. _____ You need to check your biggest bags.

11. _____ Bags can go over you and under your seat.

Letters and Sounds

◆ **Directions:** Read these words. Circle the 2 consonants at the end of each word.

1. jump

2. biggest

3. How many consonant sounds do you hear at the end of **jump**, 1 or 2? _____

4. How many consonant sounds do you hear at the end of **biggest**, 1 or 2? _____

> **TIPS:**
> ▸ The letters **mp** come together at the end of many words.
> ▸ The letters **st** come together at the end of many words.
> ▸ You can hear the sounds for both letters when you read a word that ends with **mp** or **st**.

◆ **Directions:** Read these words. Write each word in the chart where it belongs.

lamp   rest   pump

lump   damp   test

rhymes with *best*	rhymes with *jump*	rhymes with *camp*
5. _____	7. _____	9. _____
6. _____	8. _____	10. _____

◆ **Directions:** Write the letters on the lines. See how many words you can make.

d	l	b	j	p	t	w	c

11. _____ est   15. _____ ump   19. _____ amp

12. _____ est   16. _____ ump   20. _____ amp

13. _____ est   17. _____ ump   21. _____ amp

14. _____ est   18. _____ ump

Story Words

◆ **Directions:** Read each word to yourself. Then say the word out loud. Write the word on the line. Check the box after each step.

night   Read ❑ Say ❑ Write ❑ _____

parachute   Read ❑ Say ❑ Write ❑ _____
 (par | a | chute)

dark   Read ❑ Say ❑ Write ❑ _____

ground   Read ❑ Say ❑ Write ❑ _____

More Word Work

TIPS:
- ▸ Every word has at least one syllable.
- ▸ Every syllable has at least one vowel.

 one-syllable words: c l i m b   d o g   w o r l d

- ▸ Some words have more than one syllable.
- ▸ Every syllable still has at least one vowel.

 two-syllable words: b i g | g e st   r i v | e r   p a d | d l e

◆ **Directions:** Read these words. If the word has 1 syllable, write 1 on the line. If it has 2 syllables, write 2 on the line. Then circle the vowels.
Example: w a t e r _____2_____

22. acted _____   25. snap _____

23. dirt _____   26. exit _____

24. kayak _____   27. under _____

◆ **Directions:** Add **ed** to each word below. If the new word has 1 syllable, write 1 on the line. If the new word has 2 syllables, write 2 on the line.
Example: act   acted   2
      look   looked   1

28. kayak   _____ _____

29. climb   _____ _____

30. need   _____ _____

31. ground   _____ _____

NIGHT JUMP!

"Private, this is not a test. Jump out, now!"

U.S. Army Private Max Webb, 18, jumped out the back exit of the big plane. It was not his first jump, but it was his first night jump. It was dark—very dark. A big gust of air hit him as he jumped out into the night. He fell way down, way fast. He had on a parachute and ruck sack.

He felt the tug of his parachute going up. He looked about him into the damp night mist. Where was he? Six men—his buds—had jumped out of the plane. He could see dim parachutes under him in the dark. He looked up. Could parachutes be up there, as well? It was a challenge to find them in the dark. A tug on the ruck sack rig let it fall out under him. The ruck ran out to the end of a rope. He got the rope in his fist.

Quick now. Max checked about him for parachutes. Oh, man! He could see a parachute falling down at him. A quick tug on the rope let him tip his parachute. This made the parachute dip down and out of the way.

Now—where was the ground? This night was not just dark. It was filled with mist. "I can not see the ground!" Private Webb said to no one but the night air. The ground could come up fast. Then, there it was. He was just about on it. Time to jam. The ruck sack on its rope under him hit the ground. Bump! Max hit the ground and went into a roll.

Down! He was OK. Then his parachute was down. He looked about for his buds. He yelled out. They yelled back. They were on the ground. It was the first night jump for all of them, and all of them were OK.

What Do You Think?

◆ **Directions:** Do you think you would make a good paratrooper? Take this quiz to find out. Read each sentence. If it is true for you, circle **YES**. If it is not true for you, circle **NO**.

1. I am up for big challenges.   YES   NO
2. I like to work as a team.   YES   NO
3. I can follow orders.   YES   NO
4. I do not mind heights.   YES   NO
5. I like being in airplanes.   YES   NO

If you answered YES to all 5, you might like being a paratrooper. If you answered NO to all 5, this is probably not the job for you.

Think About the Story

Use Story Words

◆ **Directions:** Write a word from the box to finish each sentence.

dark	parachute	ground	night

6. Max Webb jumped out of the airplane at _____.
7. He hit the _____ as he landed.
8. The night was _____ and filled with mist.
9. Max had on a ruck sack and a _____.

When Did It Happen?

◆ 10. Write a number from 1 to 5 in front of each event to show when it happened.

_____ Max and his buds all landed OK.

_____ Max jumped out of the airplane.

_____ Max said, "I can not see the ground!"

_____ Max felt his parachute go up.

_____ Max checked about him for parachutes.

Letters and Sounds

◆ **Directions:** Read these words. Circle the 2 consonants at the end of each word.

1. hand

2. sent

3. How many sounds do you hear at the end of **hand,** 1 or 2? _____

4. How many sounds do you hear at the end of **sent,** 1 or 2? _____

> **TIPS:**
> ▸ The letters **nd** come together at the end of many words.
> ▸ The letters **nt** come together at the end of many words.
> ▸ You can hear both letter sounds when you read a word that ends with **nd** or **nt.**

◆ **Directions:** Read these words. Write each word in the chart where it belongs.

| send | sent | band |
| bent | land | mend |

rhymes with *hand*	rhymes with *went*	rhymes with *bend*
5. _____	7. _____	9. _____
6. _____	8. _____	10. _____

◆ **Directions:** Write the letters on the lines. See how many words you can make.

| s | b | t | l | h | d | r | gr |

11. _____ and

12. _____ and

13. _____ and

14. _____ and

15. _____ and

16. _____ ent

17. _____ ent

18. _____ ent

19. _____ ent

20. _____ ent

Story Words

Word Bank

Write each of these story words in the Word Bank at the back of this book.

◆ **Directions:** Read each word to yourself. Then say the word out loud. Write the word on the line. Check the box after each step.

karate (ka | ra | te) Read ❏ Say ❏ Write ❏ _____

respect (re | spect) Read ❏ Say ❏ Write ❏ _____

part Read ❏ Say ❏ Write ❏ _____

control (con | trol) Read ❏ Say ❏ Write ❏ _____

kind Read ❏ Say ❏ Write ❏ _____

body (bod | y) Read ❏ Say ❏ Write ❏ _____

used Read ❏ Say ❏ Write ❏ _____

board Read ❏ Say ❏ Write ❏ _____

More Word Work

Let's sum up what you have learned about syllables.

> ▸ Every word has at least one syllable.
> ▸ Every syllable has at least one vowel.
> ▸ Some words have more than one syllable.

◆ **Directions:** Write each word. Draw a line between the syllables. To do this, find the word and the ending. Draw a line in between them.

Example: landed   land | ed

21. handing _____   24. sending _____

22. rented _____   25. rested _____

23. camping _____   26. keeping _____

◆ **Directions:** Write each word. Draw a line between the syllables. To do this, find the two consonants in the middle of the word. Draw a line between them.

Example: bungee   bun | gee

27. biggest _____   30. under _____

28. challenge _____   31. mascot _____

29. combat _____   32. magnet _____

KARATE

What do you think of when you think about karate? Do you think of a man kicking a stack of boards into bits? Well, that is just one part of what karate is all about.

What Is Karate?

Karate is a kind of one-on-one combat. Parts of the body, like the hands and feet, can be used.

In karate you learn how to land kicks and hits. You learn how to use your body to block kicks and hits. You must learn to be very quick, as well.

Not Just Kicks and Hits

Karate is not just about being fast with your fist. It is not just about kicking boards. It is about respect. It is about keeping in control. In karate, you act with respect all the time, not just when you are doing karate.

What You Need for Karate

If you learn karate, you need a *gi*. The *gi* has a top, pants, and a belt.

You need time to spend on your skills. There is a lot to learn! You must learn to test your body and control your will. You must learn when not to hit. If you learn karate very well, you may be tested for the black belt. This is the top belt in karate. The best of the best get to be black belts.

Karate is a Japanese word. It means "empty hand."

Tae kwon do is Korean.

Kung fu is Chinese.

You Be the Judge

◆ 1. What do you think is the best thing about karate? Why?
     If you like, use these words in your answer.

control   body   learn   respect

_____

_____

Think About the Story

Use Story Words

◆ **Directions:** Write a word from the box to finish each sentence.

control	body	respect	karate	board

2. Parts of the _____ can be used in karate.

3. In karate, you must keep in _____.

4. You must act with _____ all the time.

5. You land kicks and hits in _____.

6. One thing you learn in karate is how to kick a _____.

What Are the Facts?

◆ **Directions:** Write **True** next to each sentence that is true.
   Write **False** next to each sentence that is false.

7. _____ Karate is all about kicking boards.

8. _____ You must be very quick in karate.

9. _____ A *gi* is a kind of kick.

10. _____ A red belt is the top belt in karate.

11. _____ Karate is about control and respect.

12. _____ You can learn karate fast.

Letters and Sounds

> **TIPS:**
> ▸ The letters **sh** come together at the beginning of some words. They stand for the sound you hear at the beginning of **shot**.
>
> ▸ The letters **th** come together at the beginning of some words. They stand for the sounds you hear at the beginning of **thick** and **them**.
>
> ▸ The letters **ch** come together at the beginning of some words. They stand for the sound you hear at the beginning of **chin**.

◆ **Directions:** Read these words. Circle **th, sh,** or **ch**.

1. chip   3. ship   5. thing
2. thick   4. she   6. chat

◆ **Directions:** Write each word next to the right clue.

7. not thin _____   10. not he _____

8. an object _____   11. a thin snack _____

9. what pals do _____   12. rests on water _____

◆ **Directions:** Find 3 words that begin with **sh, th,** or **ch**. Circle them. Then write them on the lines.

x	c	z	o
t	h	i	s
r	o	z	h
s	p	n	i
s	x	n	n

13. begins with **ch** _____

14. begins with **sh** _____

15. begins with **th** _____

◆ **Directions:** Say these tongue twisters. Practice saying them until you can say them fast and still get all the words right.

Shelly sells sea shells.

Shelly sells chipped sea shells to Chet.

Should Chet shell out cash for chipped sea shells? Shucks, no.

Story Words

◆ **Directions:** Read each word to yourself. Then say the word out loud. Write the word on the line. Check the box after each step.

two	Read ❑ Say ❑ Write ❑ _____
many (man│y)	Read ❑ Say ❑ Write ❑ _____
her	Read ❑ Say ❑ Write ❑ _____
by	Read ❑ Say ❑ Write ❑ _____
fight	Read ❑ Say ❑ Write ❑ _____
cool	Read ❑ Say ❑ Write ❑ _____

Word Bank

Write each of these story words in the Word Bank at the back of this book.

More Word Work

Let's sum up what you have learned about syllables.

> ▸ A word can have one or more syllables. Every syllable has at least one vowel.
>
> ▸ You can split a word into syllables in between a base word and an ending.
>
> ▸ You can split a word into syllables in between two consonants.
>
> Examples: tracking   track│ing
> biggest   big│gest
>
> ▸ A syllable can have more than one vowel letter.
>
> Example: bun│gee

◆ **Directions:** Write 1 or 2 to tell how many syllables each word has. Then write the word. Draw a line between the syllables

Example: bungee   2   bun│gee

16. grounded   _____ _____
17. falling   _____ _____
18. needed   _____ _____
19. combat   _____ _____
20. gotten   _____ _____
21. magnet   _____ _____

◆ **Directions** Circle the vowel letter or letters in each syllable you wrote.

Example: bungee   2   b(u)n│g(e e)

KARATE COOL

Dan was on his way to the hot dog stand. He had a part time job there. His shift was from 5 to 9. If the bus was on time, he could just make it by 5.

At the bus stop Dan ran into two kids. One was a big kid, Randy. Randy was the kind of kid who acted like a big shot. Plus, he could pick a fight just like that. "I could jog to the stand," Dan was thinking. But he had to be there by 5—no way could he make it.

"Hot dog man, look fast!" Randy said. Randy acted like he was doing a karate chop in the air. He acted like he was going for Dan.

"Cut it out, Randy," Dan said. He was sick of kids doing karate chops at him. Dan was a whiz at karate. He was a small kid when he first got into it. Now he was going for his black belt.

Randy did not let up. "Think you are bad?" he said. "You are not bad. You are a chump." Randy thumped Dan in the chest. Then the kid with Randy made a fist.

"Back off," Dan said. "I am not going to fight you." Just then a cop on a bike rolled up to the bus stop.

"Things OK with you kids?" she asked. Randy did not look at her. He just grunted. She shot a cool look at Randy, then at his pal.

"You two. On your way," she said. They did as she said.

The bus rolled up then, on time.

"You kept your cool," the cop said to Dan as he went to get on. "Way to go."

"That was karate cool," Dan said to her with a grin.

You Be the Judge

1. Do you think Dan did the right thing? Why or why not? Circle an answer and check a reason. Or, write your own.

YES	NO
❑ It is best to keep your cool.	❑ He acted like a wimp.
❑ He could have hurt Randy.	❑ Randy needs a karate chop or two.
❑ It is not OK to fight.	❑ Randy will keep on messing with him.
❑ _____ (your idea)	❑ _____ (your idea)

2. Write a sentence telling if Dan was right to act as he did. Tell why you think as you do.

_____

_____.

Think About the Story

Use Story Words

Directions: Write a word from the box to finish each sentence.

two	her	many	fight	cool

3. One plus one is _____.

4. Dan was not about to _____ with Randy.

5. You learn to keep your _____ in karate.

6. How _____ hot dogs did you get?

7. The cop rolled up on _____ bike.

Directions: Read the questions. Circle the answer.

8. What did Dan learn from karate?

   a. Keep your cool.

   b. Get to your job on time.

   c. Use karate first. Then chat about it.

9. What message does this story give?

   a. It is OK to fight if a cop can not see it.

   b. Do not get in a fight if you can help it.

   c. Do not go to a bus stop if Randy is about.

Chapter 3: Summary of Skills and Strategies

Let's look back at what you learned in Chapter 3.

Letters and Sounds

◆ You learned . . .

  ‣ the letters **wh** can stand for the **h** sound or the **w** sound.

  ‣ the letter **u** can stand for the short **u** vowel sound.

  ‣ the letters **qu** at the beginning of a word can stand for the **kw** sound in **quick**.

  ‣ the letter **x** at the end of a word can stand for the **ks** sound in **mix**.

  ‣ the sounds that the letters **sh, th,** and **ch** can stand **for.**

Stories and Skills

◆ You learned about . . .

  ‣ characters who learn how to do new things.

  ‣ a sub from Civil War times.

  ‣ how to keep your cool using karate.

◆ You learned . . .

  ‣ how to look ahead, or predict, what story characters might do.

Words and Meanings

◆ You learned . . .

  ‣ a lot of new words.

  ‣ some words are made up of two smaller words.

  ‣ every syllable has at least one vowel.

  ‣ how to split words into syllables.

The chapter review will give you a chance to show what you have learned.

Part A

Summing It Up: Letters and Sounds

▶ The letters **mp, st, nd,** and **nt** come together at the end of many words.

◆ **Directions:** Read these words. Write each word in the list where it belongs.

camp	best	jump	send	sand	bend
pump	hand	went	bent	ramp	west

rhymes with *rest*	rhymes with *lamp*	rhymes with *bump*
1. _____	3. _____	5. _____
2. _____	4. _____	6. _____

rhymes with *land*	rhymes with *tent*	rhymes with *mend*
7. _____	9. _____	11. _____
8. _____	10. _____	12. _____

▶ The letters **sh** stand for the sound at the beginning of **shot.**
▶ The letters **th** stand for the sound at the beginning of **them.**
▶ The letters **ch** stand for the sound at the beginning of **chin.**
▶ The letters **qu** stand for the sound at the beginning of **quick.**

◆ **Directions:** Find the word from the box that fits each clue. Write the word on the line.

quit	thin	shin	think	quick

13. not fat _____

14. You do this to learn. _____

15. to stop _____

16. on the leg _____

17. fast _____

Part B
Summing It Up: More Word Work

> ▸ You can add **s** to many words to make them tell about more than one.
> ▸ You can add **ed** to many verbs to make them tell about the past.
> ▸ You can add **ing** to many verbs to make them tell about now.

◆ **Directions:** Add an ending from the box to each word to make a word that fits in the sentence. Write the new word on the line.

s	ed	ing

1. learn   These kids are _____ karate.

2. hand   I _____ Jill a paddle.

3. ship   Two _____ went by the dock.

4. wall   How many _____ did you climb?

5. bump   A bike _____ into a rock and skidded in the mud.

6. jump   Hank is _____ off a board into the water.

7. board   Lil ran down the ramp and _____ the airplane just in time.

> ▸ Every word has at least one syllable.
> ▸ Every syllable has at least one vowel.
> ▸ Some words have more than one syllable.
> ▸ A syllable can have more than one vowel.

◆ **Directions:** Write 1 or 2 to tell how many syllables a word has. Then write the word. If it has two syllables, draw a line between the syllables.

8. handing   _____ _____

9. biggest   _____ _____

10. rested   _____ _____

11. ground   _____ _____

12. bungee   _____ _____

13. needed   _____ _____

14. used   _____ _____

15. under   _____ _____

94 *Chapter 3*

Part C

Story Words

◆ **Directions:** On the lines below, write the word from the list that matches each clue.

your	parachute	mask	exit	night
two	cool	see	part	ship

1. look _____

2. not hot _____

3. made for going on water _____

4. It is for you. _____

5. Use this to come down slow. _____

6. made to go over a face _____

7. a way out _____

8. the dark time _____

9. not all of it _____

10. one and one _____

◆ **Directions:** On the lines below, write a word from the list to finish each sentence.

year	under	time	dark
used	many	again	control

11. I will tell you when it is _____ to go.

12. Now that the sun has set, it will get _____ fast.

13. You need to _____ your bike on the track.

14. We went to the river last year, and we will go _____ this year.

15. My pal has made _____ bungee jumps.

16. A sub was picked out of the mud in the _____ 2000.

17. A torpedo runs fast _____ the water.

18. Rex _____ a rope and a carabiner to climb the wall.

Part D

Think About the Stories

Who Did What?

◆ **Directions:** This list has the names of the people who were in the stories in Chapter 3. Write a name on the line to finish each sentence.

Willis	Max Webb	Dan
Zack	Randy	

1. _____ is big and likes to pick fights.

2. _____ can kick a bag again and again.

3. _____ made a night jump with a parachute.

4. _____ will learn to kick from Zack.

5. _____ keeps cool when a kid thumps him in the chest.

◆ **Directions:** Read each sentence. If it is true, write **True** on the line. If it is false, write **False** on the line.

6. _____ Karate is just about being fast with your feet and fists.

7. _____ To learn karate, you need a *gi* on your body.

8. _____ The black belt is the top belt in karate.

9. _____ A quick tug on a rope can make a parachute dip.

10. _____ Night jumps are a snap.

11. _____ When you hit the ground at the end of a jump, you need to go into a roll.

12. _____ The *U.S.S. Housatonic* went down from a torpedo hit.

13. _____ The torpedo was shot from the *Hunley*, a sub in the Confederate Navy.

14. _____ The year of that fight was 1995.

15. _____ The sub did not make it back to Charleston.

16. _____ The *Hunley* is now in the mud where it went down in 1864.

CHAPTER 4

Lesson 1 . . . . page 98
   "In Costume," Part 1

Lesson 2 . . . . page 104
   "In Costume," Part 2

Lesson 3 . . . . page 110
   "America's Biggest and Baddest Rides"

Lesson 4 . . . . page 116
   "Girls Send Plastics Into Space"

Lesson 5 . . . . page 122
   "Take It by Skate," Part 1

Lesson 6 . . . . page 128
   "Take It by Skate," Part 2

Letters and Sounds

TIPS:

▸ The letters **sh** come together at the end of some words. They stand for the sound you hear at the end of **wish**.

▸ The letters **th** come together at the end of some words. They stand for the sound you hear at the end of **path**.

▸ The letters **ch** or **tch** come together at the end of some words. They stand for the sound you hear at the end of **such** and **patch**.

◆ **Directions:** Read these words. Circle the consonants at the end of each word.

1. match	**3.** such	**5.** with	**7.** rich
2. math	**4.** ditch	**6.** sash	**8.** hush

◆ **Directions:** Write each word from above in the chart where it belongs.

ends like *rash*	ends like *catch*	ends like *path*	ends like *much*
9. _____	**11.** _____	**13.** _____	**15.** _____
10. _____	**12.** _____	**14.** _____	**16.** _____

◆ **Directions:** Write the letters on the lines. See how many words you can make.

c	b	f	d	w

17. _____ ish	**20.** _____ ash
18. _____ ish	**21.** _____ ash
19. _____ ish	**22.** _____ ash

Word Bank

Write each of these story words in the Word Bank at the back of this book.

Story Words

◆ **Directions:** Read each word to yourself. Then say the word out loud. Write the word on the line. Check the box after each step.

call   Read ❑ Say ❑ Write ❑ _____

costume (cos│tume) Read ❑ Say ❑ Write ❑ _____

people (peo│ple)   Read ❑ Say ❑ Write ❑ _____

character   Read ❑ Say ❑ Write ❑ _____
    (char│ac│ter)

day   Read ❑ Say ❑ Write ❑ _____

cartoon (car│toon) Read ❑ Say ❑ Write ❑ _____

want   Read ❑ Say ❑ Write ❑ _____

More Word Work

◆ **Directions:** You can add **s** to many words. Add **s** to make a word tell about more than one, or to make a word tell about now.

Example: costume   costume + s = costumes

> **TIP:**   For words that end in **x, ch, tch, sh,** or **s,** add **es** instead of **s.**
>
> **Examples:**   wish + **es** = wishes
> box + **es** = boxes

◆ **Directions:** Add **es** to each word. Write the word, ending, and new word on the lines.

Example: match   match + es = matches

23. mix _____ + _____ = _____

24. itch _____ + _____ = _____

25. dish _____ + _____ = _____

26. patch _____+ _____ = _____

27. fix _____ + _____ = _____

28. rich _____ + _____ = _____

IN COSTUME, PART 1

"I need cash," said Nisha. "I wish I had a job."

"Wishes will not get you a job," said Mom. "You must go out and get one." Mom set out the *Times* for Nisha. "Look at all the jobs in these ads." Nisha looked at all the ads. Then one jumped out at her:

Cartoon Character

PART-TIME JOBS at Big America Theme Park. Six jobs in costume as cartoon characters. Must like acting. Must like people. Two + days/wk. Call Phil Nash at (455) 566-0300.

Nisha yelled out, "In costume as a cartoon character! What a kick! That is the job for me!"

Mom said, "I think you must act fast, Nisha. Lots of people will want to be a cartoon character at Big America. Can you call Mr. Nash now?"

"I can and I will," said Nisha. She went to make the call.

"This is Shelly at Big America. How may I help you?"

"Shelly, a job ad was in the *Times*, and I want to get that job," said Nisha. "Is Phil Nash in?"

"Yes, I will connect you."

"Phil Nash," said a man.

"Mr. Nash, your job ad was in the *Times*. I am Nisha Banks—I am calling about the job to be a cartoon character, in costume," said Nisha.

"Are you 16, Nisha? Can you get to Big America?"

"I am 17," said Nisha. "And I can get to Big America, no problem."

"OK, Nisha. Can you come in to Big America at 4:00? We will be seeing people about the jobs all day. Just ask for me when you get to Big America."

"You bet, Mr. Nash," said Nisha. "I will see you at 4:00."

At 4:00 Nisha went to Big America. She and about 100 people met with Phil Nash. At first Nisha did not think she could get the job, but she did! About 20 people got jobs. Some people got sales jobs. Some people got jobs as cartoon characters. Nisha was to be in costume as a cartoon character— a big duck.

The first thing she had to do was learn how to get the costume on. The costumes were all kept on a big wall. Phil called it the Costume Shop. She had to learn how to get the costume down from the wall and get into it. That was no snap! Then she had to learn how to act like a cartoon duck.

"Nisha," said Phil Nash, "Kids like the duck—lots of kids will come up to you and all the cartoon characters. You will need to be with kids all day. On this job, you cannot look mad or sad. If a kid steps on your feet or grabs your duck bill, you must be cool about it. If the day is hot, it will get very, very hot in the costume. And in the costume, you cannot see out that well. Can you do this duck costume job all day?"

"Yes, I can!" said Nisha. She got on the top part of the duck. It was big. She looked out of the costume. "Gosh," said Nisha. "It is hot in this costume. How do I look?"

Mr. Nash made one hand go up to his lips. He was telling Nisha to hush now. In costume, she was the duck, and she had to act like it.

"You look like a duck!" said Phil. "Now, can you act like one?"

Nisha ducked her duck bill up and down. She quacked. She made one or two steps like a duck.

"No quacking," said Mr. Nash. "In costume, use your body to play the part."

"OK, I got it," Nisha said. The costume was hot. But now she was the cartoon duck! She was going to like this job!

What Do You Think?

◆ 1. Do you think Nisha will like being a cartoon character at Big America Theme Park? Why or why not?

_____

_____

You will find out when you read Part 2 of "In Costume."

Think About the Story

Use Story Words

◆ **Directions:** Look at your list of story words on page 99. Write a story word on each line.

2. In a _____ you do not look like you.

3. Nisha went to _____ Mr. Nash about the job.

4. Nisha and Mr. Nash are two _____.

5. The _____ Nisha will play is a duck.

6. You can see a _____ on TV.

7. If it is not night, it could be _____.

8. Do you _____ to get a job?

When Did It Happen?

◆ 9. Write a number from 1 to 5 in front of each event to show when it happened.

_____ Nisha puts on the duck costume.

_____ Nisha looks at ads to find a job.

_____ Nisha calls Mr. Nash.

_____ Nisha quacks like a duck.

_____ Nisha goes to Big America at 4:00.

Write Sentences About the Story

◆ **Directions:** Read the job ad that Nisha looked at. Answer the questions with information in the ad.

10. How many days a week is the job at Big America?

   _____

   _____

11. How many jobs are there as cartoon characters?

   _____

   _____

12. What skills does someone need for the job?

   _____

   _____

13. What is the name of the job?

   _____

   _____

Why Did It Happen?

◆ **Directions:** Draw a line from each event to the reason it happened.

What Happened	Why
14. Nisha calls Mr. Nash at Big America.	○ Nisha needs cash.
15. Nisha wishes she had a job.	○ Nisha gets the job as a cartoon character.
16. Nisha puts on the costume and acts like a duck.	○ Nisha reads an ad for a job at Big America.

Letters and Sounds

> **TIPS:** ▸ The letters **nk** stand for one sound—the sound you hear at the end of **think.**
>
> ▸ The letters **ng** stand for one sound—the sound you hear at the end of **ring.**

◆ **Directions:** Read these words. Circle **ng** or **nk.**

1. think	3. went	5. sung	7. ink
2. hung	4. hand	6. bent	8. sand

◆ **Directions:** Find 4 sets of words from above that rhyme. Write them on the lines.

9. _____   and   10. _____

11. _____   and   12. _____

13. _____   and   14. _____

15. _____   and   16. _____

◆ **Directions:** Write the letters on the lines. See how many words you can make.

th	g	j	l	s	t	tr	r

17. _____ ank   20. _____ unk   23. _____ ing   26. _____ ong

18. _____ ank   21. _____ unk   24. _____ ing   27. _____ ong

19. _____ ank   22. _____ unk   25. _____ ing   28. _____ ong

Word Bank

Write each of these story words in the Word Bank at the back of this book.

Story Words

◆ **Directions:** Read each word to yourself. Then say the word out loud. Write the word on the line. Check the box after each step.

there   Read ❑ Say ❑ Write ❑ _____

put   Read ❑ Say ❑ Write ❑ _____

more   Read ❑ Say ❑ Write ❑ _____

sound   Read ❑ Say ❑ Write ❑ _____

some   Read ❑ Say ❑ Write ❑ _____

heavy (heav│y)   Read ❑ Say ❑ Write ❑ _____

More Word Work

◆ **Directions:** Read each clue. Think of the missing word. Write letters on the lines to finish the words.

Example: when a ship goes down   s   i   nk

29. where the cash is   ___ ___ nk

30. what you sing   ___ ___ ng

31. what an airplane has   ___ ___ ng ___

32. a camp bed   ___ ___ nk

33. where dishes go   ___ ___ nk

34. what you do when you get a gift   ___ ___ ___ nk

35. game you play with a paddle   ___ ___ ng ___ ___ ng

IN COSTUME, PART 2

The next day, Nisha went to Big America. "Now I am Nisha," she said. "But on the job I will be the duck!" Nisha looked up at the sun. The day was hot.

She went to the Costume Shop and put on the duck costume. She sank down under the top of the costume. "I did not think it was going to be this heavy," she said.

"All set to go out there and be with the people, Nisha?" asked Phil Nash. "I will put you out there with the 3 pigs at first. The kids will all run to see you. Just act like a duck with them. I will hang back to see how you do. It is 10:00 now. I will come back to check on you at 10:15. You will be out till 11:30, and then off for a bit. Then you will go out some more, from 11:30 to 12:00."

"OK and thank you," said Nisha. From under the costume, it sounded like, "Mmm-mm, Mmm-mm-mmm." That was the last sound that Nisha could make.

She and the 3 pigs went out into the Park. Many, many people were there. The sun was hot, and the costume got hot fast. The air in the costume—well, there was not much! Nisha looked out from the costume, but could not see very well. She did her best to get some air.

People were thrilled to see the duck and the pigs. Kids ran up to them fast. Some kids went to hug the duck. Nisha did not see them come up. They bumped into her. She just about fell down. One kid went to tug on the costume.

"I must be a duck—I cannot get mad. I cannot make a sound—not a quack!" Nisha said. She lifted up her duck wings. She put them on the kids in a big hug. A band was playing a song. Nisha made the duck costume go this way and that. She ducked her duck bill up and down. Tunk! Tunk! She acted like a duck. The 3 pigs ducked up and down with Nisha. All the kids liked it. They went this way and that to the song with the duck and the pigs. It was fun!

As the day went on, it got hot hot HOT in the sun. The costume got as heavy as a rock. Nisha was all wet in the duck costume. She had bumped about for a long time as this duck. It was not as fun as it had been at first. When was Phil going to come and get them?

"The duck! The duck!" yelled some kids. Nisha did not like the sound of more kids. They ran up for a hug. Nisha could not see well at all. Now she could not see the 3 pigs. She had lost them in all the people. Where was she? Where were the pigs? Where was a map? Where was Phil? What if Phil could not find her?

"Help!" Nisha wished she could run back to the Costume Shop and get out of the costume. Water ran down her back and legs. She could not see a thing. She was way hot. The costume was way heavy. "Quack! I think there are way many kids!" she said to herself.

But she had to keep on being the duck. She made her wings go up and down. She made her duck bill bob up and down. She made herself hug all the kids. She did not make a sound. She could not see just where she was, but she kept going all about Big America.

Then she felt a tap on her back. It was Phil. He said, "There you are, duck! I was looking for you! How about if you come with me now?"

He put his hand on her wing and led her back to the Costume Shop. At last, there were no more kids. Nisha got the costume off fast.

Phil handed her some water. "Thanks," she said. "How did I do? I could not find the 3 pigs. I was lost!"

"Well, you were out there for a long time!" said Phil. "The 3 pigs went in at 10:30. Now it is 11:00. I think you did more than OK on your first day!"

What Do You Think?

◆ 1. Would you like to have a job as a cartoon character in a costume? Why or why not? If you like, use some of these words in your answer.

hot	kids	cool	fun
quack	acting	think	people

_____

_____

_____

_____

Think About the Story

Use Story Words

◆ **Directions:** Look at the list of story words on page 105. Write a word on each line.

2. The costume was very _____.

3. As a duck, Nisha did not make a _____.

4. Nisha kept cool when _____ kids bumped into her.

5. Phil said, "_____ you are, duck."

6. Nisha was glad when there were no _____ kids.

7. Nisha _____ on the duck costume.

What's the Big Idea?

◆ 8. Which sentence tells what the whole story is about? Write it on the lines.

   a. At Big America, people dress up as ducks and pigs.

   b. Nisha does well on her first day on the job.

   c. The duck costume was very heavy.

_____

_____

_____

When Did It Happen?

◆ **9.** Write a number from 1 to 4 in front of each event to show when it happened.

_____ Nisha hugs kids with her duck wings.

_____ Phil tells Nisha she did OK on her first day.

_____ Nisha gets hot and the costume gets heavy.

_____ Phil taps Nisha on the back.

Write Sentences About the Story

◆ **Directions:** Use words from the story to answer these questions.

10. What is it like for Nisha inside the duck costume?

_____

_____

11. How does Nisha have to act when she is in costume?

_____

_____

12. Do you think Nisha is glad when Phil finds her? Why or why not?

_____

_____

Letters and Sounds

> **TIP:** ▸ When the same two consonants come together at the end of a word, they stand for one sound. **Less** ends with the **s** sound. **Wall** ends with the **l** sound. **Buzz** ends with the **z** sound.

◆ **Directions:** Circle the consonants at the end of each word. Write the sound you hear at the end of each word.

Example: le(ss)   s

1. miss _____   3. buzz _____   5. egg _____

2. mitt _____   4. off _____   6. odd _____

◆ **Directions:** Write the letters on the lines. See how many words you can make.

k	l	gr	b	m	f	dr

7. _____ iss   9. _____ess   12. _____ uzz

8. _____ iss   10. _____ ess   13. _____ uzz

                   11. _____ ess

14. _____ uff   16. _____ ill

15. _____ uff   17. _____ ill

                   18. _____ ill

◆ **Directions:** Write a word from the box on each line.

pill	buzz	fuzz
mess	hiss	bluff

19. Some bugs do this. _____

20. A chick has this. _____

21. A mad cat makes this sound. _____

22. This is a hill. _____

23. This can help if you are sick. _____

24. You make this if you drop an egg. _____

Story Words

Directions: Read each word to yourself. Then say the word out loud. Write the word on the line. Check the box after each step.

wood	Read ❑ Say ❑ Write ❑	_____
steel	Read ❑ Say ❑ Write ❑	_____
ride	Read ❑ Say ❑ Write ❑	_____
roller coaster	Read ❑ Say ❑ Write ❑	_____
(rol|ler coast|er)		

Word Bank

Write each of these story words in the Word Bank at the back of this book.

More Word Work

Directions: You know you can add **es, ed,** and **ing** to many words. Add **es, ed,** and **ing** to these words. Write the new words on the lines.

Example: fizz   fizzes   fizzed   fizzing

	es	ed	ing
25. dress	_____	_____	_____
26. miss	_____	_____	_____
27. buzz	_____	_____	_____

TIPS:
  ▸ Add **s** to words that end in **ll** or **ff**.
  ▸ Add **es** to words that end in **zz** or **ss**.

Directions: Add **s** or **es** to each word. Write the new word on the line.

28. bluff _____   **31.** fizz _____

29. mess _____   **32.** buzz _____

30. pill _____   **33.** cuff _____

AMERICA'S BIGGEST AND BADDEST RIDES

Are you a fan of roller coasters? These days, over 50 big roller coasters are put up in a year. One coaster, "The Chang," in Louisville, Kentucky, you stand up to ride! It is 4,155 feet long. It gets people to 5 Gs as it hits 3 loops and two twists. Check out these roller coasters—they are some of America's biggest, baddest rides.

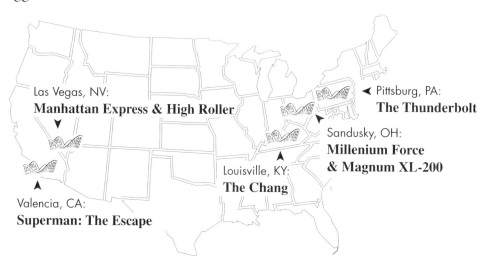

Las Vegas, NV:
Manhattan Express & High Roller

Pittsburg, PA:
The Thunderbolt

Sandusky, OH:
Millenium Force & Magnum XL-200

Louisville, KY:
The Chang

Valencia, CA:
Superman: The Escape

First "Jet Plane Roll" Twist and Drop: To ride "The Manhattan Express," you go up 205 feet, then fall into twists, hit a drop of 144 feet, and go into a last twist of 540°—all going as fast as 67 mph!

First to Go Over 200 Feet: The "Magnum XL-200" was the first big roller coaster to climb over 200 feet. It goes up at a 60° tilt, then whips down at up to 72 mph! Some people think it is the #1 steel roller coaster.

High Roller: The "High Roller" is in Las Vegas, Nevada. It sits up 900 feet high and goes 30 mph.

Big and Fast: "The Millennium Force." The Cedar Point Amusement Park in Ohio has 14 roller coasters. In the year 2000, it rolled out its biggest (310 feet in the air), fastest (93 mph), longest (6,595 feet) roller coaster of all, called "The Millennium Force." Its first drop is 300 feet!

First Coaster to Top 100 mph: Do you like torpedo rides? Then this roller coaster is for you. "Superman: The Escape" is a steel ride that has just one big drop of 415 feet. When it drops, it goes over 100 mph!

Best Wood Roller Coaster: "The Thunderbolt" was one of the first coasters. It was put up over 70 years back. It has an end drop of 90 feet—not bad for wood.

What Do You Think?

◆ 1. Which roller coaster sounds like fun to you? Why? Write your answer. Use words from the story.

_____

_____

_____

Think About the Story

Use Story Words

◆ **Directions:** Look at your list of story words on page 111. Write a word for each clue.

2. This is not made by people. _____

3. This goes up slow but comes down fast. _____

4. You sit when you do this. _____

5. People make this in big mills. _____

Where in the World Is It?

◆ 6. Write the number of each roller coaster in the map. Show about where in the U.S. each roller coaster is.

1. "The Millennium Force"
2. "High Roller"
3. "Superman: The Escape"
4. "The Thunderbolt"
5. "The Chang"

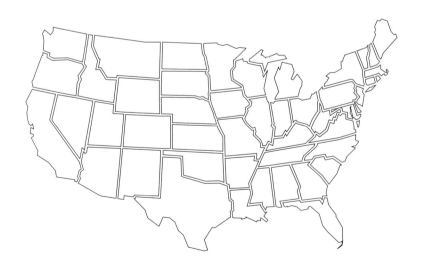

What Are the Facts?

◆ **Directions:** Draw a line to match each big roller coaster with the fact that tells about it.

7. "The Thunderbolt"　　○ This one was the first to climb over 200 feet.

8. "Magnum XL-200"　　○ You stand up to ride this one.

9. "Manhattan Express"　　○ This one has big twists.

10. "The Chang"　　○ This one is made of wood.

What's the Big Idea?

◆ 11. Which sentence tells what the story is mostly about? Write it on the lines.

　　a. Over 50 big roller coasters are put up in a year.

　　b. "The Chang" gets people to 5Gs as it hits 3 loops.

　　c. These rides are some of the biggest, baddest roller coasters in America.

　　d. Roller coasters have cool names, like "Magnum XL-200."

_____

_____

_____

Letters and Sounds

> **TIPS:** ▸ You have learned that two consonants can come together at the beginning of a word. Many blends have the letter **r** in them.
>
> ▸ When a word begins with an **r** blend, you can hear the sound of the **r** and the sound of the other consonant.

◆ **Directions:** Read these words. Circle the **r** blend at the beginning of each.

1. brick   3. crash   5. drop   7. frank
2. ground   4. print   6. trim   8. bring

◆ **Directions:** Add an **r** blend to each group of letters to make a new word.

| br | cr | dr | gr | tr |

9. _____ ash   11. _____ op   13. _____ im
10. _____ ash   12. _____ op   14. _____ im

◆ **Directions:** Make a new word by adding an **r** to the beginning of each word after the first letter. Write the new word on the line.

Example: cash   *crash*

15. dip _____   18. tack _____
16. cop _____   19. fill _____
17. tend _____   20. tick _____

Story Words

◆ **Directions:** Read each word to yourself. Then say the word out loud. Write the word on the line. Check the box after each step.

would   Read ❏ Say ❏ Write ❏ _____

different   Read ❏ Say ❏ Write ❏ _____
    (dif|fer|ent)

which   Read ❏ Say ❏ Write ❏ _____

girls   Read ❏ Say ❏ Write ❏ _____

oxygen (ox|y|gen)   Read ❏ Say ❏ Write ❏ _____

contaminate   Read ❏ Say ❏ Write ❏ _____
    (con|tam|i|nate)

contamination   Read ❏ Say ❏ Write ❏ _____
    (con|tam|i|na|tion)

space   Read ❏ Say ❏ Write ❏ _____

Word Bank

Write each of these story words in the Word Bank at the back of this book.

More Word Work

You have learned that you can add **ed** and **ing** to many verbs. What happens when you add **ed** and **ing** to a word like **grab**? Here's what happens:

$$grab + \textbf{ed} = grabbed$$
$$grab + \textbf{ing} = grabbing$$

21. What letter was added to **grab** when these endings were added? _____

> **TIP:** ▸ When adding **ed** or **ing** to a word with a short vowel sound that ends in one consonant, double the last consonant.

◆ **Directions:** Add **ed** and **ing** to each word below. Double the last consonant when you add the ending. Write the new words on the lines.

	ed	ing
22. trip	_____	_____
23. drop	_____	_____
24. fan	_____	_____
25. pad	_____	_____

GIRLS SEND PLASTICS INTO SPACE

What do you think about going up into space? For many people, going to space would be one grand trip. What if you could not go into space, but you could send up a thing that you made?

For some girls at Hathaway Brown School in Ohio, sending things into space is not just a wish. In the 1990s, Hathaway Brown girls went to the NASA John H. Glenn Research Center in Cleveland. They wanted to do a test in space, and they had a plan for what kind of test to do. They planned to send plastics into space to test them.

Test Plastics? For What?

Plastics are used for different things in space. The problem is, some kinds of plastic last a long time in space. Others do not. What plastics are the best for use in space? That is what the girls wanted to find out. The test they planned would bring about 40 kinds of plastic into space. The plastics would be made into one-inch disks. All the disks would be tested to find out which plastics do best in space.

The Plan

The Space Test, Part 1: The first part of the plastics-in-space test tracks what oxygen will do to the 40 plastics. Oxygen is in the part of space that is close to the Earth. When oxygen comes into contact with some things, it rots them over time. The girls and NASA are looking for plastics that oxygen can not rot.

The plastics-in-space testing gang at the Glenn Research Center in Cleveland, Ohio.

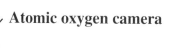

Erosion samples   **Atomic oxygen camera**

Contamination samples   **Contamination camera**

The Space Test, Part 2: The next part of the test is about what things in space contaminate the plastics. Contamination is like dirt. Some plastics may do well at keeping out contamination. But, some plastics may not. This part of the space test will help NASA find out what things contaminate plastic, and which plastics are best at keeping out contamination. Plastic disks are used in this part of the test, as well.

Tracking Oxygen Rot and Contamination

In space, snapshots will be made of the disks over time. By looking at the snapshots, NASA and the girls can track how fast oxygen rots a kind of plastic. They can track what kinds of contamination get to that plastic, and they can track how fast the contamination gets into the plastic.

What the Girls Think

How fun is all this space stuff? The girls do not think it is a drag. They like going to the NASA Center. They are doing a job that could help in space someday. It could help find the plastics that will last for a long time in space.

Check Out the Space Tests

The first test was sent into space in July of 2001. At that time, NASA planned to send the next test up in about a year. How are the plastics doing? Which ones are rotting fast? Visit the Hathaway Brown–NASA Web site to find out.

You Be the Judge

◆ 1. The girls from Hathaway Brown wanted to do something important for NASA and the world. Do you think the plastics tests are important? Why or why not?

_____

_____

_____

Think About the Story

Use Story Words

◆ **Directions:** Look at your list of story words on page 117. Write a story word on each line.

2. The _____ of the Hathaway Brown School went to NASA.

3. NASA does tests in _____.

4. They _____ test how plastics held up in space.

5. They wanted to find out _____ plastics held up best.

6. In space, _____ in the air can rot plastic.

7. Plastic has many _____ uses.

◆ **Directions:** Write **True** next to each item that is true. Write **False** next to each item that is false.

8. _____ The girls of Hathaway Brown got to go up into space.

9. _____ There are many different kinds of plastic.

10. _____ NASA stands for "Not a Sand Ant."

11. _____ The girls will take part in two tests.

12. _____ Oxygen is good for plastic.

What's the Big Idea?

◆ **13.** Which sentence best sums up the story? Write it on the lines.

    a. Some plastics will rot in space.

    b. NASA sends many things into space for testing.

    c. NASA and the Hathaway Brown girls sent plastics into space to test them.

_____

_____

_____

Write Sentences About the Story

◆ **Directions:** Use words from the story to answer these questions.

14. What did the girls want to know about plastics in space?

_____

_____

_____

15. What happens in the first part of the space test?

_____

_____

_____

16. What happens in the next part of the space test?

_____

_____

_____

Letters and Sounds

◆ **Directions:** These words have the short **a** vowel sound. Circle the vowel in each word.

1. mad   2. cap

These words have the long **a** vowel sound. Circle the two vowels in each word.

3. made   4. cape

5. What vowel do you see at the end of **made** and **cape**? _____

TIPS: ▸ The letter **a** can stand for more than one sound. It can stand for the short **a** sound in **mad,** or the long **a** sound in **made.**

▸ Words that have the **a**-consonant-**e** pattern usually have the long **a** sound.

◆ **Directions:** Read these words. Circle the words that have the short **a** sound. Draw a line under the words that have the long **a** sound.

Example: (can)   cane

6. fad   8. rate   10. tap   12. sane

7. fade   9. rat   11. tape   13. sand

◆ **Directions:** Write each word from above in the chart where it belongs.

short *a*	long *a*
14. _____	18. _____
15. _____	19. _____
16. _____	20. _____
17. _____	21. _____

◆ **Directions:** Write the letters on the lines. See how many words you can make.

t	b	h	f	m	c	s	st

22. _____ ake   25. _____ ale   28. _____ ane   31. _____ ate

23. _____ ake   26. _____ ale   29. _____ ane   32. _____ ate

24. _____ ake   27. _____ ale   30. _____ ane   33. _____ ate

Story Words

Word Bank

Write each of these story words in the Word Bank at the back of this book.

◆ **Directions:** Read each word to yourself. Then say the word out loud. Write the word on the line. Check the box after each step.

me   Read ❏ Say ❏ Write ❏ _____

been   Read ❏ Say ❏ Write ❏ _____

their   Read ❏ Say ❏ Write ❏ _____

great   Read ❏ Say ❏ Write ❏ _____

city (cit | y)   Read ❏ Say ❏ Write ❏ _____

pay   Read ❏ Say ❏ Write ❏ _____

shoes   Read ❏ Say ❏ Write ❏ _____

More Word Work

TIPS:

▸ The word **mat** has the consonant-vowel-consonant, or CVC, pattern. Words with the CVC pattern usually have a short vowel sound.

▸ The word **mate** has the consonant-vowel-consonant-**e**, or CVC**e**, pattern. Words with this pattern usually have a long vowel sound.

C	V	C
m	a	t

C	V	C	*e*
m	a	t	e

◆ **Directions:** Read these words. Write each word in the grid where it belongs.

tape   fat   pan   rat

fate   pane   rate   tap

	C	V	C
34.			
35.			
36.			
37.			

	C	V	C	*e*
38.				
39.				
40.				
41.				

TAKE IT BY SKATE, PART 1

Jake and Kate had been on their skates all day. They had been all over the city and back. They had made up skate tricks, jumps, and spins. They had been to the skate path by the lake. At last they were about to fade.

Kate flopped down on the grass in some shade. "What a great day," she said. "I wish I could spend all my days this way. But I must get a job. I need to make some cash. In no time, I will be on the job and not on skates. It makes me sad."

Jake looked over at her. "What if you could make cash on your skates?" he said. "What if you and I could find a job we could do on skates?"

"Jake," said Kate, "This is no time to play games. I need a job."

"Chill, Kate!" said Jake. "A plan is rolling. Just hang on a sec and let it come to me." Then he said, "What if we could pick things up for people? This is a big city. Lots of people need to get things to people. We could save them time. They would like that. I think people would pay us for it!"

"You are a great sales man, Jake," said Kate. "And I am your first sale! Yes, I think we could do it. I think people would pay us. What can we call this job?"

"How about 'Take It by Skate'?" said Jake. "It is fitting, is it not?"

Do you think people will pay Kate and Jake to take things by skate? Circle your answer.   YES   NO

Keep reading to find out what happens.

The next day, Jake and Kate set out to find people to skate for. They went from shop to shop. At the cake shop, they got their first job. The girl in the shop gave them two cakes in boxes. "Take these over to a shop about six blocks over, at 415 Grant. Then come back for your pay," said the girl. "And do not drop the cakes!"

Like two torpedoes, Jake and Kate dashed down the city blocks with the cakes. They made it to 415 Grant in no time flat. They sped back to the cake shop, and the girl gave them two $5 bills.

"Can we take more cakes for you?" asked Jake.

"Come back at 1 p.m.," said the girl, "I will send more cakes with you."

"Thanks," said Jake and Kate. They kept going up the block to the next set of shops.

At the pet shop, they got their next job from Mr. Webb. "I need you to take this dog basket to 15th and West," said Mr. Webb. He looked at their skates. "Will it be safe on skates? It may be best to take off the skates," he said.

The dog basket was big. It would take two to lift it. "I think skates will be OK," said Jake. "I will take this end, and Kate will take that one."

"OK," said the man. "Be quick about it, but do not drop the basket!"

Kate and Jake were off like a flash. They went about two blocks. The basket was big and heavy. They were going kind of fast. "Kate!" said Jake. "This block has a big hill!"

Kate was going fast down the hill and could not stop. She held on to her end of the basket. "Look out, Jake!" she yelled. A bike was on the pavement at the end of the block. Jake and Kate grabbed the dog basket. They spun out at the same time to miss the bike. No! They could not stop and ran into the bike. The basket went up in the air and crashed to the ground. The top of the basket was crushed.

Stunned, Kate and Jake skidded to a stop. "Now what do we do?" Kate asked Jake.

You Be the Judge

◆ 1. Kate and Jake crushed the basket they were taking for Mr. Webb.
       Do you think they should keep taking things by skate, or should
       they think of other ways to do the job? Write what you think on
       the lines below.

       _____

       _____

       _____

Think About the Story

Use Story Words

◆ **Directions:** Look at your list of story words on page 123. Write a
   story word on each line.

   2. Kate and Jake like to skate all over the _____.

   3. Will Mr. Webb _____ them to take the dog basket?

   4. Kate thinks Jake is a _____ sales man.

   5. What do you think of _____ plan?

   6. Skate next to _____.

   7. Kate and Jake had _____ all over the city.

   8. You must take off your _____ to put on skates.

When Did It Happen?

◆ 9. Write a number from 1 to 5 in front of each event to show
       when it happened.

       _____ Kate and Jake take cakes to 415 Grant.

       _____ Kate tells Jake she needs to get a job.

       _____ Kate and Jake meet Mr. Webb at the pet shop.

       _____ Jake makes up a plan called "Take It by Skate."

       _____ Kate and Jake drop the dog basket and crush it.

Write Sentences About the Story

◆ **Directions:** Use words from the story to answer these questions.

10. How does Jake think he and Kate can make cash?

_____

_____

_____

11. What is their first job? How does it go?

_____

_____

_____

12. What is their next job? How does it go?

_____

_____

_____

What's the Big Idea?

◆ **13.** Which sentence tells what the story is mostly about? Circle it.

    a. Making fast cash is a snap.

    b. Do not take dog baskets by skate.

    c. Kate and Jake get their first jobs on skates.

Letters and Sounds

> **TIP:** ▸ You have learned that two consonants can come together at the beginning of a word. Many blends have the letter **l** in them. When a word begins with an **l** blend, you can hear the sound of the other consonant and the sound of the **l**.

◆ **Directions:** Read these words. Circle the **l** blend at the beginning of each.

1. click	3. plant	5. blimp	7. clam
2. slam	4. glum	6. flop	8. pluck

◆ **Directions:** Add an **l** blend to each group of letters to make a new word.

cl	pl	sl	fl	bl

9. _____ ap	12. _____ ink	15. _____ unk
10. _____ ap	13. _____ ink	16. _____ unk
11. _____ ap	14. _____ ink	17. _____ unk

◆ **Directions:** Make a new word by adding an **l** after the first letter in each word. Write the new word on the line.

Example: cash   *clash*

18. panting _____	22. pane _____
19. cap _____	23. gum _____
20. sap _____	24. fatten _____
21. sink _____	25. puck _____

Story Words

◆ **Directions:** Read each word to yourself. Then say the word out loud. Write the word on the line. Check the box after each step.

have	Read ❑ Say ❑ Write ❑ _____
write	Read ❑ Say ❑ Write ❑ _____
each	Read ❑ Say ❑ Write ❑ _____
know	Read ❑ Say ❑ Write ❑ _____
work	Read ❑ Say ❑ Write ❑ _____
too	Read ❑ Say ❑ Write ❑ _____

Word Bank

Write each of these story words in the Word Bank at the back of this book.

More Word Work

◆ **Directions:** Adding **e** to a word like **glad** changes the vowel sound from short to long. Add **e** to these words. Write each new word on the line.

Example: glad   glade

26. plan   _____   **28.** rat   _____

27. cap   _____   **29.** man   _____

You know that you can add **ed** to many words. How do you add **ed** to a word that ends in **e**? Here is how:

skate + **ed** = skated

30. What letter was dropped from the word **skate** when **ed** was added? _____

> **TIP:** ▸ When adding **ed** to a word that ends in **e,** drop the **e.** Then add the ending.

◆ **Directions** Add **ed** to each word. First drop the **e.** Then add the ending.

Example: tame   tamed

31. frame   _____   **34.** rate   _____

32. bake   _____   **35.** fake   _____

33. stake   _____   **36.** hate   _____

TAKE IT BY SKATE, PART 2

"Jake, what will happen to us now?" said Kate. She rubbed her hand where the bike had slapped into it. "That bike clipped me. The basket is all mashed in."

"One thing I know," said Jake. "Mr. Webb will not like this. And this is going to cost us some bucks, too. We may as well write off the profits from this job!"

They grabbed the basket and skated up the hill. This time, they did not skate at all fast. They huffed and puffed to get the basket back to the pet shop. As they slid past the glass, Mr. Webb looked at the basket. "You kids," he said. "You do not know what you are doing. Can you pay for this basket? It costs $50."

Kate and Jake blinked. It would take them a long time to get $50. Kate was brave about it. "Mr. Webb, we do not have the $50 now. But will you let us work for you to make it up to you?"

"Yes. We will take a basket to 15th and West, if you have one," said Jake.

"I have one. But I will not let you take it by skate," said Mr. Webb.

Jake and Kate gulped. They would have to take off their skates. It would take them some time to do the job. "OK," they said. Their shoes were in their packs. They slipped off their skates and slid into their shoes. Mr. Webb gave them a different dog basket . They plodded the ten blocks to 15th and West with it. The people there were glad to get the basket. Then something happened that Jake and Kate did not expect. One man handed Jake a $10 tip!

Do you think Kate and Jake will make the 50 bucks? Circle your answer.   YES   NO

Keep reading to find out what happens.

"That was great," said Kate, as they left. "I did not think about getting tips! If we can make tips, it will not take as long to pay for the dog basket."

"Yes," said Jake, "but now we have to slide. It is 12:30. We have to make it back to Mr. Webb and get to the cake shop by 1:00." Their shoes flapped on the pavement as they ran all the way to the pet shop.

Mr. Webb was glad to see them. They handed over the $10 tip to him. He was glad about that, too. He got out a pad to write on. "I will keep track of your work on this pad. I will take $5 off your tab each time you take something for me. When is the next time you can come?"

"We will check in with you each day," said Kate. She looked at Jake to see if that was OK with him. He nodded. "We would like to do more now, but we have to get to the cake shop. Thanks, Mr. Webb."

This day was full of things Jake and Kate did not expect. At the cake shop, the girl had a great big wedding cake for them to take. The cake was as big as Kate, and it was very heavy. "Can you do it?" asked the girl.

Jake looked at Kate. Then they got down and slipped off their skates. No way could they skate with that cake. And they were not about to flub this job. "Uh…Kate," said Jake. "I…think we need a wagon for this job."

Kate grinned at Jake. "I have one," she said. "We can get it and come back."

The next days were filled with learning how to do their job. Some things could go by skate. That was fast and fun. Big, heavy things had to go by wagon. They rigged their bikes with baskets. The bike baskets worked best for some things. They had to find what worked for each job—skates, wagon, or bikes.

"Now we are set," said Kate, "but we have to get a name that fits. We cannot be 'Take It by Skate.' Now we are 'Take It Safe and Fast'!"

You Be the Judge

◆ 1. Do you think the job that Jake and Kate made up could work in real life? Why or why not?

_____

_____

_____

Think About the Story

Use Story Words

◆ **Directions:** Look at your list of story words on page 129. Write a word on each line to finish each sentence.

2. You _____ with a pen.

3. I _____ two tickets to the game.

4. A word for a job is _____.

5. I _____ what I am doing!

6. You can _____ take one muffin.

7. Hal likes snakes, and I like them, _____.

When Did It Happen?

◆ 8. Write a number from 1 to 5 in front of each event to show when it happened.

_____ Mr. Webb sees the crushed basket.

_____ Kate and Jake name their job "Take It Safe and Fast."

_____ Mr. Webb asks for $50.

_____ Kate and Jake take a wedding cake by wagon.

_____ Jake gets a $10 tip.

What Are the Facts?

◆ **Directions:** Write **True** next to each item that is true. Write **False** next to each item that is false.

9. _____ Mr. Webb was not upset about the basket.

10. _____ Mr. Webb said he will not give them any more jobs.

11. _____ Kate and Jake took a wedding cake by skate.

12. _____ Kate and Jake will take things by skates, wagon, or bikes.

What's the Big Idea?

◆ 13. Which sentence tells what the story is mostly about? Write it on the lines.

    a. Skates are not a good way to take cakes.

    b. Kate and Jake learn the best ways to do their job.

    c. Kate and Jake have to pay Mr. Webb $50.

_____

_____

_____

Chapter 4: Summary of Skills and Strategies

Let's look back at what you learned in Chapter 4.

Letters and Sounds

◆ You learned . . .

- the sounds that the letters **nk** and **ng** stand for.
- the letter **a** can stand for the long **a** vowel sound.
- words that have the **a**-consonant-**e** pattern usually have the long **a** sound.

Stories and Skills

◆ You learned about . . .

- characters who get jobs and make up their own jobs.
- some of the biggest roller coasters in America.
- a cool experiment that takes place in space.

◆ You learned . . .

- how to look ahead, or predict, what story characters might do.

Words and Meanings

◆ You learned . . .

- a lot of new words.
- that sometimes you can add **es** to a word to tell about more than one.
- that some words change when you add an ending.
- about the consonant-vowel-consonant, or CVC, pattern and the consonant-vowel-consonant-**e,** or CVC**e,** pattern.

The chapter review will give you a chance to show what you have learned.

Part A

Summing It Up: Letters and Sounds

> ▶ The letters **sh** stand for the sound at the end of **wish**.
> ▶ The letters **th** stand for the sound at the end of **path**.
> ▶ The letters **ch** stand for the sound at the end of **such**.
> ▶ The letters **tch** stand for the sound at the end of **patch**.
> ▶ The letters **nk** stand for the sound at the end of **think**.
> ▶ The letters **ng** stand for the sound at the end of **ring**.

◆ **Directions:** Read these words. Write each word in the list where it belongs.

bath	hutch	crash	with	drink	much
thank	rich	bang	lung	catch	fish

Ends like *dash*	Ends like *math*	Ends like *such*
1. _____	3. _____	5. _____
2. _____	4. _____	6. _____

Ends like *pitch*	Ends like *sank*	Ends like *sing*
7. _____	9. _____	11. _____
8. _____	10. _____	12. _____

> ▶ When two consonants come together at the end of a word, they stand for one sound.

◆ **Directions:** Read these words. Write each word in the list under the word it rhymes with.

fuzz	ball	pass	will
less	gruff	bell	miss

tall	hiss	dress	drill
13. _____	15. _____	17. _____	19. _____

fluff	buzz	glass	yell
14. _____	16. _____	18. _____	20. _____

> ▸ The letter **a** can stand for more than one sound. It can stand for the short **a** sound in **mad,** or the long **a** sound in **made.**
>
> ▸ Words that have the **a-consonant-e** pattern usually have the long **a** sound.

◆ **Directions:** Read these words. Write each word in the list where it belongs.

shape	flap	fate	snap
tale	ham	chat	state
pal	rate	snake	sad

short *a*	long *a*
21. _____	27. _____
22. _____	28. _____
23. _____	29. _____
24. _____	30. _____
25. _____	31. _____
26. _____	32. _____

> ▸ Two consonants can come together at the beginning of a word.
>
> ▸ When a word begins with an **r** blend, you can hear the sound of the **r** and the sound of the other consonant.
>
> ▸ When a word begins with an **l** blend, you can hear the sound of the **l** and the sound of the other consonant.

◆ **Directions:** Make a new word by adding an **r** or an **l** to the beginning of each word after the first letter.

33. sip_____   37. bag _____

34. tack _____   38. tip _____

35. cub _____   39. sick _____

36. back _____   40. cab _____

Part B

Summing It Up: More Word Work

> ▸ Add **s** to make a word tell about more than one, or to make a word tell about now. For words that end in **x, ch, tch, sh, s, ss,** or **zz,** add **es** instead of **s.**

◆ **Directions:** Add **s** or **es** to each word. Write the new word on the line.

1. box _____
2. miss _____
3. ship _____
4. cuff _____
5. crash _____
6. rope _____
7. patch _____

8. bed _____
9. rich _____
10. grub _____
11. bluff _____
12. dress _____
13. mill _____
14. fizz _____

> ▸ Words with the consonant-vowel-consonant-pattern, or CVC pattern, usually have a short vowel sound.
> ▸ Words with the consonant-vowel-consonant-**e** pattern usually have a long vowel sound.

◆ **Directions:** Read these words. Write each word in the grid where it belongs.

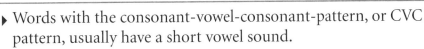

| **late** | **red** | **cape** |
| **hide** | **zip** | **nap** |

	C	V	C
15.			
16.			
17.			

	C	V	C	*e*
18.				
19.				
20.				

> When adding **ed** or **ing** to a word with a short vowel sound that ends in one consonant, double the last consonant.

◆ **Directions:** Add **ed** and **ing** to each word below. Double the final consonant when you add the ending.

	ed	ing
21. slip	_____	_____
22. pat	_____	_____
23. beg	_____	_____
24. drop	_____	_____

Part C

Story Words

◆ **Directions:** On the lines below, write the word from the list that matches each clue.

some	space	costume	day
pay	**more**	**know**	**shoes**
write	**wood**	**oxygen**	**roller coaster**

1. Do this with a pen. _____
2. Get this for working. _____
3. Learn it. _____
4. not a lot, but more than one _____
5. need this in your lungs _____
6. a stick, a board _____
7. way out there _____
8. takes you on a fast ride _____
9. for feet _____
10. Use this to look different. _____
11. not less _____
12. not night _____

◆ **Directions:** On the lines below, write a word from the list to finish each sentence.

have	call	ride
too	character	steel
different	sound	great
girls	heavy	city

13. Lil made a _____ play to win the game.

14. Nisha was a cartoon _____ in "In Costume."

15. She got _____ hot in her costume.

16. Which pal would you _____ first?

17. Do you _____ a lot of work to do?

18. The _____ of the big drum woke me up.

19. Would you _____ on the biggest roller coaster?

20. _____ is used to make airplanes.

21. All the _____ had on red dresses.

22. That big rock must be very _____.

23. About 100,000 people come to the _____ to work every day.

24. Chet asked for the same thing, but what he got was _____.

Part D

Think About the Stories

Who Did What?

◆ **Directions:** This list has the names of the people who were in the stories in Chapter 4. Write a name on the line to finish each sentence.

Jake   Nisha   Mr. Webb

Kate   Phil Nash

1. _____ acted like a duck.

2. _____ had a wagon for big, heavy things.

3. _____ met with people who wanted to be cartoon characters.

4. _____ was handed a $10 tip.

5. _____ got mad when he looked at the mashed-in basket.

◆ **Directions:** Read each sentence. If it is true, write **True** on the line. If it is false, write **False** on the line.

6. _____ There is a roller coaster you ride standing up.

7. _____ No roller coaster whips down at more than 67 mph.

8. _____ Las Vegas, NV, has two big roller coasters.

9. _____ The biggest, fastest roller coaster at Cedar Point Amusement Park is "The Thunderbolt."

10. _____ If you hate torpedo rides, you will like "Superman: The Escape."

11. _____ For girls, sending things into space is just a wish.

12. _____ Some plastics do not last a long time in space.

13. _____ There is no oxygen close to the Earth.

14. _____ The girls from Hathaway Brown are helping NASA learn about contamination of plastics.

15. _____ The girls from Hathaway Brown will go up in a space ship to test plastics.

CHAPTER 5

Lesson 1 . . . . page 142
  "Up in Smoke," Part 1

Lesson 2 . . . . page 148
  "Up in Smoke," Part 2

Lesson 3 . . . . page 154
  "What Are You Putting in Your Body?"

Lesson 4 . . . . page 160
  "Beep Me!" Part 1

Lesson 5 . . . . page 166
  "Beep Me!" Part 2

Lesson 6 . . . . page 172
  "Number Games"

Letters and Sounds

◆ **Directions:** These words have the short **o** sound. Circle the vowel letter in each word.

1. not

2. rock

These words have the long **o** sound. Circle the two vowel letters in each word.

3. note

4. rope

5. What vowel letter did you circle at the end of **note** and **rope**? _____

TIPS: ▸ The letter **o** can stand for the short **o** sound in **not,** or the long **o** sound in **note.**

▸ A word that has the **o**-consonant-**e** pattern usually has the long **o** sound.

◆ **Directions:** Read these words. Circle the words that have the short **o** sound. Draw a line under the words that have a long **o** sound.

Example: (not)   note

6. hop	8. cope	10. stock	12. rode
7. hope	9. cop	11. stoke	13. rod

◆ **Directions:** Write each word below in the chart where it belongs.

pond	came	lamp	gate
cans	tone	drop	hope

short *o*	long *o*	short *a*	long *a*
14. _____	16. _____	18. _____	20. _____
15. _____	17. _____	19. _____	21. _____

◆ **Directions:** Write the letters on the lines. See how many words you can make.

p	st	ch	h	z	b

22. _____ oke	25. _____ ole	28. _____ one
23. _____ oke	26. _____ ole	29. _____ one
24. _____ oke	27. _____ ole	30. _____ one

Word Bank

Write each of these story words in the Word Bank at the back of this book.

Story Words

◆ **Directions:** Read each word to yourself. Then say the word out loud. Write the word on the line. Check the box after each step.

cigarette (cig | a | rette) Read ❑ Say ❑ Write ❑ _____ _____

so Read ❑ Say ❑ Write ❑ _____

who Read ❑ Say ❑ Write ❑ _____

friend Read ❑ Say ❑ Write ❑ _____

turned Read ❑ Say ❑ Write ❑ _____

other (oth | er) Read ❑ Say ❑ Write ❑ _____

school Read ❑ Say ❑ Write ❑ _____

More Word Work

Let's sum up what you have learned about vowel patterns:

▸ The words **can, rack,** and **crop** have the consonant-vowel-consonant pattern. Most words with CVC have a short vowel sound.

▸ The words **cane** and **hope** have the consonant-vowel-consonant-**e** pattern. Most words with CVC**e** have a long vowel sound.

◆ **Directions:** Read these words. Write each word in the right list.

| chat | smoke | top | fate |
| joke | lock | name | pan |

CVC	CVC*e*
31._____	35. _____
32. _____	36. _____
33._____	37. _____
34._____	38. _____

◆ **Directions:** Add the ending **ed** to each word below. Double the final consonant for CVC words. Drop the final **e** for CVC**e** words. Write the new word on the line.

Examples: dim *dimmed* tame *tamed*

39. sip _____ 42. bake _____

40. note_____ 43. hop _____

41. pop _____ 44. joke _____

Use What You Know

Have your friends ever bugged you to do something you really did not want to do? How can you say "no" to friends who pressure you? Write your answer on the lines below. Then read to see what Clarice does when two friends try to get her to smoke cigarettes.

_____

_____

_____

UP IN SMOKE, PART 1

"Drat! I am out of matches," said Rob. "Clarice, do you have some? Or what about you, Brent?"

"Nope," said Clarice. "You know I do not bring matches with me."

"I may have some in my other pocket," said Brent. "Who knows what is down there!" He fished down into a pocket and got out a small pack of matches. "Got some!" he said. He struck one and held it up for Rob. He put the end of a cigarette into the flame and sucked in some air. Brent got out a cigarette and lit up, too.

Clarice turned to keep her nose out of the way of the smoke. She did not like to inhale that stuff. But the thick smell of cigarette smoke filled the air. Each day it was the same thing. They went home from school with each other. Just as they got off the school grounds, Brent and Rob lit up. It made her mad, but they were her friends. So she **kept cool** about it.

"So, when are you going to have a smoke with us, Clarice?" asked Brent. "It is not such a big thing, is it? Stop being such a snob, girl!"

"So who are you, my boss?" said Clarice, keeping her tone flat. At times her friends made fun of her for not smoking cigarettes with them. "I do not like smoke in my lungs. Smoke is bad for your body—I know that. You know it, too."

Brent and Rob did not press her more. Who knows what they were thinking? Did she have to smoke, just to be friends with them? All of a sudden Rob said, "I need to get home. See ya!"

Do you think Clarice will try smoking cigarettes? Circle your answer.

YES   NO

Read on to find out what happens next.

Clarice and Brent gave him a wave and kept going. In two more blocks, Brent turned down D Street. "See you," he said. Clarice was **bummed.** Other than the cigarette thing, she liked Brent and Rob. They had been close friends for such a long time.

When she got home, Clarice ran up the steps. Her mom yelled out, "Is that you, Clarice? I am so glad you are home. Something bad has happened to Uncle Albert. He has had a stroke! Clarice, he may not last the night. Your dad is with him now, but it may be the last time we see him."

"Is this a joke, mom?" asked Clarice. With one look at her mom, Clarice could tell it was no joke. Not Uncle Albert! He was so much fun that she could not think of him as other than up and well. Clarice broke down. "Mom," she sobbed, "How did this happen? Can we see him?"

"Yes, your dad would like us to come down as fast as we can. But Uncle Albert may not wake up when we are there. You know, I think all the years he smoked played a big part in this. I kept telling him time and again to quit. Now it is so sad…." She put her hands over her face.

On the way to see Uncle Albert, Clarice could not help thinking about Rob and Brent. They did not know what they were doing. How could they? She could not help thinking about all the smoke that was going into their lungs. She wished she could get them to stop. Plus, she was sick of being the odd one out all the time. She was sick of them **bugging her.** "I may have to look for other friends," she was thinking.

You Be the Judge

◆ 1. Should Clarice look for new friends just because the friends she has smoke cigarettes? Write your opinion. If you like, use these words in your answer.

choice   boss   bad   body

_____ _____

_____

_____

Think About the Story

Use Story Words

◆ **Directions:** Look at your list of story words on page 143. Write a story word on each line.

2. You learn things at _____.

3. I left my cash in my _____ pants.

4. A _____ will help you if you ask.

5. Put that _____ out! It is bad for your lungs!

6. Jen _____ left at the end of the block.

7. Jake wants to know _____ that girl is.

8. I am late, _____ I will run.

When Did It Happen?

◆ 9. Write a number from 1 to 4 in front of each event to show when it happened.

_____ Clarice thinks, "I may have to look for other friends."

_____ Brent asks Clarice to have a smoke.

_____ Clarice finds out her uncle Albert had a stroke.

_____ Clarice tells her friends that smoking is bad for the body.

Words and Meanings

◆ **Directions:** Think about how the **bold** words are used in the story. Then circle the words that show the meaning of each word or phrase.

10. Clarice **kept cool.** This means she _____.
    a. did not get hot
    b. did not get upset
    c. kept out of the sun

11. Clarice was **bummed.** This means she was _____.
    a. out of cash
    b. late
    c. sad

12. In this story, **bugging her** means _____.
    a. watching her
    b. making her mad
    c. putting bugs in her bag

Write Sentences About the Story

◆ **Directions:** Use words from the story to answer these questions.

13. Why does Clarice think cigarettes are not for her?

    _____ _____

    _____ _____

14. How does Clarice feel when she finds out about Uncle Albert?

    _____ _____

    _____

15. Do you think Clarice will ask Brent and Rob to stop smoking?

    _____

    _____

Look Ahead

16. Do you think Clarice will keep Rob and Brent as friends? Circle a prediction.

    YES   NO

Read Part 2 of "Up in Smoke" to find out.

Letters and Sounds

> **TIPS:** ▸ You know that two consonant letters often come at the beginning of a word. The letter **s** is part of many consonant blends.
>
> ▸ In a word that starts with an **s** blend, you can hear the sound of the **s** and the sound of the other consonant letter.

◆ **Directions:** Read these word pairs. Circle the word in each pair that has the **s** sound and another consonant sound at the beginning.

Example: (still)   shall

1.	stone	shone	**4.**	smell	shell
2.	ship	stick	**5.**	stack	shack
3.	snake	shake	**6.**	skim	shin

◆ **Directions:** Add **s** blends to the lines. Make words that fit the rhymes.

Example: I can s t and
       on one hand.

7. That red ___ ___ake
    is as thin as a rake.

8. Make a ___ ___ack
    in the back.

9. Be ___ ___ill,
    if you will.

10. That big shell
    has an odd ___ ___ell.

◆ **Directions:** Read these words. Write each word in the list where it belongs.

sticks   fish   ships
shacks   bricks   steps
clams   snakes   shells

what you see in water	what you see on land
11. _____	**15.** _____
12. _____	**16.** _____
13. _____	**17.** _____
14. _____	**18.** _____
	19. _____

Story Words

Word Bank

Write each of these story words in the Word Bank at the back of this book.

◆ **Directions:** Read each word to yourself. Then say the word out loud. Write the word on the line. Check the box after each step.

number (num│ber)   Read ❏ Say ❏ Write ❏ _____

listen (lis│ten)   Read ❏ Say ❏ Write ❏ _____

began (be│gan)   Read ❏ Say ❏ Write ❏ _____

or   Read ❏ Say ❏ Write ❏ _____

talk   Read ❏ Say ❏ Write ❏ _____

hot line   Read ❏ Say ❏ Write ❏ _____

tobacco (to│bac│co)   Read ❏ Say ❏ Write ❏ _____

More Word Work

You know that you can add **ing** to many words. Here is how to add **ing** to a word that ends in **e**:

make + ing = making

What letter was dropped from the word **make** when **ing** was added? _____

TIP: ▸ When adding **ing** to a word that ends in **e**, drop the **e**. Then add the ending.

◆ **Directions:** Add **ing** to each word below. Write the new word on the line.

Example: close   *closing*

20. skate _____ _____

21. slope _____ _____

22. rate _____ _____

23. bake _____ _____

24. pose _____ _____

25. trade _____ _____

26. doze _____ _____

27. hose _____ _____

UP IN SMOKE, PART 2

Clarice and her mom and dad spent a lot of the night sitting by Uncle Albert. He was under an oxygen tent and they could not talk with him. He would get over this stroke. But no one could say if he would be the same again. Clarice kept thinking about her friends. She did not want them to end up with strokes or other problems. But what was the use? They would not listen to her.

The next day, Clarice got to talking with other people at school. She was shocked to find that many of them felt as she did about cigarettes. Some kids had lost people who were close to them. Clarice began to make friends with a girl named Susan, and with some others. As they talked, they began to think of things they could do to get kids to stop smoking.

One day Susan and Clarice came up with a plan. They went to talk to Principal Stone. "We would like to do something about kids who smoke," Susan said. We think a number of them would quit if they could get help. We could set up a hot line number for kids who want to quit but need help doing it."

"Girls, this sounds like a great plan," said Principal Stone. "I would like to help you. Tell me more about it. How would you run the hot line?"

"We could get an 800 or 900 number," said Clarice. "We would have to get some cash to pay for that. I think my mom and dad would help out. Or we could have a bake sale. Kids from school could take calls at night. If we could just get six or ten people to run the hot line, it could work."

Do you think the hot line plan will work? Circle your answer.

YES   NO

Read on to find out what happens.

"Yes," said Susan, "and we can plan a 'quit smoking' day. We could call it Just Quit Day. We could set up a spot where kids could find out about the problems that can come from using tobacco. We could match people up with each other. Then they could help each other quit."

Clarice jumped in. "If we could get kids to call the hot line each time they felt like picking up a cigarette, it could help them quit."

"I like your plan, girls," said Principal Stone. "And I will be glad to help get this going on campus. Let me look into a good date for a Just Quit Day."

The plan began to roll. The date for Just Quit Day was set. Clarice, Susan, and a number of their friends began making up fact kits on tobacco use. They began taking names for the hot line. They held a contest for kids to make up the best Just Quit ads.

On Just Quit Day, something happened that Clarice and her friends did not expect. People from TV Channel 6 came out to the school. Principal Stone had called them. They filmed what was happening and put it on TV that night.

The hot line began to ring! So many kids called. They were not just from the school. Kids called from all over the city. Susan, Clarice, and the others spent lots of time talking and listening to all the kids who called. When a call came in from Rob, Clarice was jazzed.

"I am so glad you called," said Clarice. "And keep calling!" Rob did keep calling. With help, he quit smoking, too.

"Want a job?" Clarice asked Rob one day. "We could use your help on the hot line."

So Rob staffed the hot line, as well. For Clarice, the best part was not just getting more hands to help. The best part was getting a friend back.

What Do You Think?

◆ 1. What kind of hot line would you set up to help people in your school? Your hot line could be for helping people kick bad habits. Or it could have a different use, such as:

- home work help
- dating tips
- night life tips for kids
- help with finding a job, or keeping one

Write your hot line idea here.

_____ _____

_____

_____ _____

Think About the Story

Use Story Words

◆ **Directions:** Look at the list of story words on page 149. Write a word on each line.

2. One is a _____, and so is two.

3. You can call a _____ for help.

4. Kids _____ with friends after school.

5. Vinny likes to_____ to jazz.

6. I _____ _____ to munch chips and I could not stop.

7. Do you like clams _____ not?

8. Cigarettes are made from _____.

When Did It Happen?

◆ 9. Write a number from 1 to 5 in front of each event to show when it happened.

_____ Clarice went to see her uncle Albert.

_____ Rob quit smoking.

_____ People from TV Channel 6 came to film Just Quit Day.

_____ Clarice and Susan talked to Principal Stone about their plan for a hot line.

_____ Rob staffed the hot line with Clarice.

What Are the Facts?

◆ **Directions:** Write **True** next to each item that is true. Write **False** next to each item that is false.

10. _____ Principal Stone did not like the plan about the hot line.

11. _____ Clarice and Susan made up fact kits on tobacco use.

12. _____ No one called the hot line.

13. _____ Rob and Clarice quit being friends.

What's the Big Idea?

◆ 14. Which sentence best sums up this part of the story? Write it on the lines.

    a. Clarice had a great plan to help kids stop smoking.

    b. Clarice got Rob to stop smoking.

    c. Clarice and Susan got put on TV Channel 6.

_____

_____

_____

Letters and Sounds

◆ **Directions:** These words have the long **e** sound you hear in **need.** Circle the vowel letter or letters in each word. Then write the vowel letters.

1. me _____

2. seed _____

3. mean _____

TIPS: ▸ The letter **e** can stand for the short **e** sound in **get,** or the long **e** sound in **need.**

▸ The letters **e, ee,** and **ea** can stand for the long **e** sound.

◆ **Directions:** Read these words. Circle the words that have the long **e** sound.

4. she	7. bead	10. deed
5. pen	8. went	11. were
6. he	9. be	12. sea

◆ **Directions:** Write the letters on the lines. See how many words you can make.

b	f	sh	m	k	d

13. _____ eet   17. _____ eep   21. _____ e

14. _____ eet   18. _____ eep   22. _____ e

15. _____ eet   19. _____ eep   23. _____ e

16. _____ eet   20. _____ eep

◆ **Directions:** Circle 4 words with the long **e** sound. Write the words on the lines.

p	x	o	s
h	e	a	t
e	x	o	e
n	x	o	a
t	e	a	m

24. _____

25. _____

26. _____

27. _____

Story Words

◆ **Directions:** Read each word to yourself. Then say the word out loud. Write the word on the line. Check the box after each step.

word	Read ❏ Say ❏ Write ❏ _____
oil	Read ❏ Say ❏ Write ❏ _____
alcohol (al | co | hol)	Read ❏ Say ❏ Write ❏ _____
warning (warn | ing)	Read ✓ Say ✓ Write ✓ _____warning_____
food	Read ✓ Say ✓ Write ✓ _____food_____
good	Read ✓ Say ✓ Write ✓ _____good_____
health	Read ❏ Say ❏ Write ❏ _____
serving size (serv | ing size)	Read ❏ Say ❏ Write ❏ _____
label (la | bel)	Read ❏ Say ❏ Write ❏ _____

More Word Work

◆ **Directions:** Read these word pairs. If the words sound the same, circle **YES.** If they do not sound the same, circle **NO.**

28. see   sea   YES   NO

29. meet   meat   YES   NO

> **TIP:** Some words sound the same, but have different meanings.
> ▸ **See** means "to look."
> ▸ **Sea** means "a big body of water."
> To tell which meaning a word has, look at the other words in the sentence.

◆ **Directions:** Write a word from the box to finish each sentence.

| beat | beet | reel | real |

30. I _____ the rug to get it clean.

31. Dee cut up a _____ and put it on a plate.

32. Small kids think monsters are _____.

33. I got a new fishing _____ for my dad.

Use What You Know

What kinds of foods are good for your health?

_____   _____

What kinds of foods are bad for your health?

_____

WHAT ARE YOU PUTTING IN YOUR BODY?

You have just one body. It is up to you to keep it working well. If you keep fit and eat well, you could get to be 100. What you put into your body has a lot to do with how you feel. It has a lot to do with how long you will keep in good health. If you keep putting in junk and gunk, you will end up feeling like, well, junk. You see, bad stuff adds up over time in the body. So what kinds of things are like junk for the body? Tobacco, drugs, alcohol, and junk foods are the big things that can make people sick over time.

Tobacco: Tobacco smoke has over 40 things in it that can kill you or make you very sick. Plus, tobacco products cost you a lot of cash—over $4 for just one pack of cigarettes. So think long about keeping tobacco out of your body. Just in case you still think tobacco is OK, think about this: All tobacco products must have printed warning labels on them. Would this be so if they were safe to use?

| WARNING: This product may cause mouth cancer. |

| SURGEON GENERAL'S WARNING: Tobacco Seriously Damages Health. |

Alcohol: It is a sad thing that many tobacco and alcohol ads appeal to teens. If a teen gets into the habit of using tobacco and drinking alcohol, then he or she may spend a lot of cash on tobacco and alcohol products for many years. Warning labels help teens know what risks they run from the use of alcohol.

| GOVERNMENT WARNING: Drinking alcoholic beverages impairs your ability to drive a car or operate machinery, and may cause health problems. |

Junk Foods: What are junk foods? They are foods your body does not need and can not use well. Many teens like foods that are made with lots of sweets or oils. Oils are fats. Pop, chips, and fast foods are just some kinds of junk food. To keep in good health, it is best to limit the fats and sweets that you take in. Food labels tell you what is in food products. Did you know that just one can of pop has about 1.5 times the sweets your body needs in a day?

Food Labels—Do the Math: The words on food labels are complex. Some labels can be tricky to read. This label came from a bag of chips. It was not a big bag, but the kind you could get for a snack. These steps will help you read the label.

1. Find where the label lists grams of fat. How many grams are listed? _____.

2. Find the serving size. How many chips are in one serving? _____.

3. How many servings are in the bag? _____.

Are you thinking, "get real"? Who eats just 1/3 of a bag of chips? So, do the math. From just one bag of chips, you get:

calories: 130 x 3 = _____

fats: 10g x 3 = _____

The chips in the bag have about 1/2 of the fat that is OK for you to eat in a whole day. Snacks like that are not the best thing to put in your body day after day.

Nutrition Facts		
Serving Size 1 oz. (about 10 chips)		
Servings Per Container about 3		
Amount Per Serving		
Calories 130	Calories from Fat 90	
		% Daily Value
Total Fat 10g		17%
Saturated Fat 1.5g		8%
Cholesterol 0mg		0%
Sodium 170 mg		7%
Total Carbohydrate 24g		8%
Dietary Fiber 6g		24%
Sugars 4g		
Protein 6g		
Vitamin A 2%	•	Vitamin C 0%
Calcium 0%	•	Iron 6%
* Percent Daily Values are based on a 2,000 calorie diet.		

What Do You Think?

◆ 1. What is one healthy snack or drink you like a lot? Write it here.

_____

_____

2. What is one unhealthy snack or drink you think you should maybe have a little less of? Write it here.

_____

_____

Think About the Story

Use Story Words

◆ **Directions:** Look at your list of story words. Write a word on each line for each clue.

3. means "look out"   _____

4. tells what is inside   _____

5. a kind of fat   _____

6. a drink that can make you sick _____

7. what we eat   _____

8. means "great"   _____ _____

9. how much you eat at one time _____

10. how well you are   _____

11. part of a sentence   _____

What's the Big Idea?

◆ 12. Which sentence tells what the story is about? Write it on the lines.

   a. Food labels can trick you into eating too much.

   b. Tobacco, alcohol, and junk food can be bad for your body.

   c. Cigarettes cost a lot of cash.

_____

_____

Find the Facts

◆ **Directions:** Look at the chart and then answer the questions.

The Food Pyramid

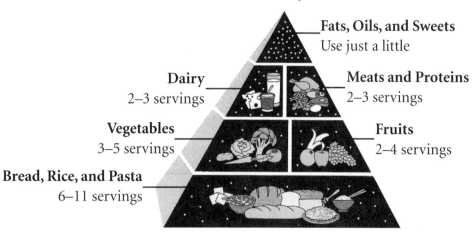

13. What should you eat the most of?

_____

14. How many servings of fruit should you eat in a day?

_____

15. How much fats, oils, and sweets should you have?

_____

Write Sentences About the Story

◆ **Directions:** Use words from the story to answer these questions.

16. What are some ways in which tobacco is bad for you?

_____

_____

17. How can food labels sometimes be tricky to read?

_____

_____

18. Why is junk food not healthy for you?

_____

_____

Letters and Sounds

◆ **Directions:** These words have the short **i** sound. Circle the vowel letter in each word.

    1. tin   **2.** sip

These words have the long **i** sound. Circle the two vowel letters in each word.

    3. like   **4.** time

    5. What vowel letter do you see at the end of **like** and **time**? _____

TIPS: ▸ The letter **i** can stand for the short **i** sound in **tin,** or the long **i** sound in **like.**

         ▸ Words that have the **i**-consonant-**e** pattern usually have the long **i** sound.

◆ **Directions:** Read these words. Circle the words that have the short **i** sound. Draw a line under the words that have the long **i** sound.

Example: (sip)   like

    6. pin   **8.** dime   **10.** slim   **12.** fine

    7. pine   **9.** dim   **11.** slime   **13.** fin

◆ **Directions:** Write each word from above in the chart where it belongs.

short *i*	long *i*
14. _____	**18.** _____
15. _____	**19.** _____
16. _____	**20.** _____
17. _____	**21.** _____

◆ **Directions:** Write the letters on the lines. See how many words you can make.

t	n	h	f	m	d	s	sl

    22. _____ ine   **26.** _____ ide

    23. _____ ine   **27.** _____ ide

    24. _____ ine   **28.** _____ ide

    25. _____ ine   **29.** _____ ide

Story Words

◆ **Directions:** Read each word to yourself. Then say the word out loud. Write the word on the line. Check the box after each step.

any (a|ny)	Read ❏ Say ❏ Write ❏	_____
busy (bus|y)	Read ❏ Say ❏ Write ❏	_____
beeper (beep|er)	Read ❏ Say ❏ Write ❏	_____
message (mes|sage)	Read ❏ Say ❏ Write ❏	_____
new	Read ❏ Say ❏ Write ❏	_____
mall	Read ❏ Say ❏ Write ❏	_____

Word Bank

Write each of these story words in the Word Bank at the back of this book.

More Word Work

◆ **Directions:** Add **ing** to each word. Write the new word on the line. (Hint: Drop the **e** with CVCe words. Double the final consonant with CVC words.)

Examples: time *timing*   jump *jumping*

30. like _____   **38.** note _____

31. raft _____   **39.** skate _____

32. use _____   **40.** mine _____

33. smile _____   **41.** wish _____

34. dim _____   **42.** plan _____

35. ride _____   **43.** hide _____

36. slide _____   **44.** line _____

37. tap _____   **45.** brim _____

Use What You Know

Have you ever seen a beeper, also called a pager? How do you use a beeper?

_____

_____

The next story is about a kid who gets a new beeper. He thinks the beeper will make a girl like him. Read to see what happens.

BEEP ME! PART 1

Adam slipped the new green beeper out of its packet. He looked at it with pride. "David," he said to his best friend, "at last I am up-to-date. I have a beeper now. And just look at this. It came with a list of beeper codes. Now I think Mina will talk to me. She is into beepers big time. This beeper is my **ticket** to a date. I will just go up to her and take out my cool new beeper. Then I will ask her out."

"Mina will not have time to talk to you," said David. "She is too busy."

But Adam was **off in space**. He went on and on about Mina and the beeper. "Just think about it. Mina will send me beeper messages. It would be cool to get my first message from Mina. Then I will buzz her back. Best of all, David, now I will know where she is. With this beeper, I have a hot line to catch up with her any time."

"Adam," said David, "you may have a beeper, but I do not think you can catch up with Mina. That girl has so much going on, no one can find her. She is coming and going so fast that she meets herself on the way!"

The next day at school, Adam was riding on a tide of good feelings. He went up to Mina and gave her a wide smile. "Hey, Mina, what is up with you?" He spoke fast to keep her listening. "See my new beeper?" He flashed the green beeper. "Do you like it? Where is yours? We could send messages to each other! Which makes me think…how about if you and me go hang out at the mall when school gets out?"

Do you think Mina will meet Adam after school? Circle your answer.

YES   NO

Read on to find out what happens.

Mina gave him a quick smile. "Cool beeper," she said. She looked up at the big campus clock. "Listen, Adam, I have a meeting to go to now." She turned to run off. Adam, loping fast to keep up, stuck by her side.

"Mina! Will you meet me at the city mall when you get out of school?" he said. "What is your beeper number? Or do you need mine?"

Mina looked back but did not stop. "Adam, I am kind of busy now."

Adam got out a pen fast. "Write your beeper number on my hand," he said. "It will not take any time." Good. Mina stopped, grabbed the pen, and jotted a number on his hand. He hoped the oil on his skin would not keep the pen from writing. It worked. "Mina, do you have something I can write my number on?"

She flipped out a note pad. Writing as fast as he could, he put down ten numbers. He hoped she could make them out when she had time to look at them.

"OK," she said, and began to run again. "Time to go!"

The bell rang. A tide of kids coming out of class swept Mina up.

"Mina!" yelled Adam. "What time?—at the mall—what time?"

Craning her neck to see him past all the kids, Mina looked back. "I will beep you," she yelled. "Do you know the codes?"

"What?" yelled Adam.

"Beeper talk—you know, codes!"

Adam gave her a big nod yes. Good thing he had the beeper code list. He was all smiles. He had a date with Mina. She was going to beep him!

You Be the Judge

1. Some people have cell phones, beepers, pagers, lap tops, and all kinds of other gadgets. Do you think people have too many gadgets? Check your answer.

   ❏ too many gadgets

   ❏ just the right amount

   ❏ not enough gadgets

2. If you checked "too many gadgets," which ones do you think we could do without?

   _____ _____

   _____

Think About the Story

Use Story Words

◆ **Directions:** Look at your list of story words on page 161. Write a story word on each line.

3. A _____ is filled with shops.

4. Take a _____ _____ for me.

5. I can call you on your _____ _____.

6. You must rip the tag off those _____ parts.

7. I am too _____ _____ to play catch now.

8. Do you have _____ _____ cash?

Words and Meanings

◆ **Directions:** Think about how the **bold** words are used in the story. Then circle the words that show the meaning of each word or phrase.

9. Adam thinks the beeper is his **ticket** to a date. This means _____.

   a. the beeper will get him a free plane ticket

   b. he thinks it is the way for him to get a date

   c. the beeper looks like a ticket

10. Adam was **off in space**. This means _____.

    a. he was not listening to David

    b. he was on a space ship

    c. he was walking down the hall

Why Did It Happen?

◆ **Directions:** Draw a line from each event to the reason it happened.

11. Adam shows Mina his new beeper.

12. Adam is all smiles.

13. Mina has to run off quickly.

○ Mina said she would beep him.

○ Mina is very busy.

○ Adam thinks Mina will go out with him after she sees his beeper.

Write Sentences About the Story

◆ **Directions:** Use words from the story to answer the questions.

14. What does David say about Mina?

_____ _____ _____

_____ _____

15. Do you think Mina wants to go out with Adam? Why or why not?

_____ _____

_____ _____

16. How will Mina tell Adam what time to meet her?

_____ _____

_____

Look Ahead

◆ 17. Do you think Mina will beep Adam? Will she meet him at the mall? Write a prediction. Then read Part 2 of "Beep Me!" to see if you are right.

_____ _____ _____

_____

_____

Letters and Sounds

◆ **Directions:** Read these words. Circle the words that end with the **s** sound.

1. face   2. rock   3. space   4. sock

5. What two letters do the words you circled end with? _____

> **TIP:** ▸ Many words end with the letters **ce.** The letters **ce** usually stand for the **s** sound.

◆ **Directions:** Read these words. Circle the words that end with the **s** sound at the end of **face.**

6. race   8. slice   10. bake

7. snap   9. check   11. rice

◆ **Directions:** Write the letters on the lines. See how many words you can make.

| n | | f | | r | | tw | | pl |

12. _____ ice   15. _____ ace

13. _____ ice   16. _____ ace

14. _____ ice   17. _____ ace

◆ **Directions:** Add letters to lines. Make a word that fits each clue.

Example: means "two times"   t w ice

18. where a rocket goes   _____ ____ ace
19. what a thing costs   ____ _____ ice
20. a running match   _____ ace
21. fast or slow   ___ ace
22. to cut up   _____ ____ ice
23. what your nose is on   _____ ace
24. a good food   _____ ice

Story Words

◆ **Directions:** Read each word to yourself. Then say the word out loud. Write the word on the line. Check the box after each step.

figure (fig│ure)   Read ❏ Say ❏ Write ❏ _____

read   Read ❏ Say ❏ Write ❏ _____

after (af│ter)   Read ❏ Say ❏ Write ❏ _____

hospital (hos│pi│tal) Read ❏ Say ❏ Write ❏ _____

hello (hel│lo)   Read ❏ Say ❏ Write ❏ _____

Word Bank

Write each of these story words in the Word Bank at the back of this book.

More Word Work

Let's sum up what you have learned about adding endings to words.
- ▸ You can add **ed** and **ing** to many verbs.
- ▸ When you add **ed** or **ing** to a word with a short vowel sound that ends with a single consonant, double the final consonant.
- ▸ When you add **ed** or **ing** to a word that ends in **e,** drop the **e.**

Examples: nod   nodded   nodding

race   raced   racing

◆ **Directions:** Add **ed** and **ing** to each word below. Write the new words on the lines.

Example: bake   baked   baking

	+ ed	+ ing
25. hum	_____	_____
26. face	_____	_____
27. tame	_____	_____
28. trace	_____	_____
29. pad	_____	_____
30. smile	_____	_____

BEEP ME! PART 2

After school, Adam went to get his backpack. When he turned, he was face to face with David. "Good news!" Adam said. "Mina is going to meet me at the mall! Come with me, will you?"

"Like I said," said David, "I think she is way busy. She will not make it."

"Yes, she is busy. But she said she would beep me with the time she can meet. So it is all set up. Just come with me, OK?"

"OK, bud," said David. "Did you get her number, too?"

"What do you think I am, a dope?" said Adam. "Yes, I got it."

Adam and David rode the bus to the mall. For a while, they went into shops they liked. They listened to some CDs. Adam looked at the clock. It was past five, and Mina still had not beeped him. He began to fret. "Do you think I need to beep her?" he said. Just then his beeper buzzed.

"Cool!" he said. "My first message!"

Numbers flashed on the beeper. It was the number Mina gave him. After her beeper number were the numbers 07734* 1-4-1-13.

"It is from Mina!" said Adam. "She is sending me a message in code! She must be on her way. All I have to do is figure out what these numbers mean."

"So how are you going to do that?" said David.

"I have this list of beeper codes. I just have to read the numbers on the list." He got out the list. "See, number one is A and number two is B. I get it."

A B C D E F G H I J K L M N O P Q R S T U V W X Y Z
1 2 3 4 5 6 7 8 9 10 11 12 13 14 15 16 17 18 19 20 21 22 23 24 25 26

Adam began to read the code list…"07734 would be…G-G-C-D!"

"I do not get this at all!" said David. "G-G-C-D?"

"But see, this one spells my name," said Adam. "1-4-1-13 … A-D-A-M!"

Just then the beeper buzzed again. More numbers flashed: **87*-123-101.** Adam looked down the other part of the list. It had sets of numbers with messages by them. "87—OK, that stands for the word *fun*. And *123*—yes, it is…*milk*. And *101*—that one is…*hospital!*"

"*Fun, milk,* and *hospital?* Is she joking with you?" said David.

Adam did not know what to think. "I hope she is OK! David, do you think we need to go to the hospital to find her?"

Do you think Mina is messing with Adam? Circle your answer.

YES   NO

Read the rest of the story to "get the 411."

"Adam! David! Hello, you two!" It was Mina. She ran up to them. "Adam, did you get my beeper messages?"

"Yes…kind of," Adam said. "But what was that about milk and the hospital? And what does *07734* stand for?"

"*07734* means 'hello.' You did not know that? See, the * means you have to turn it up side down. Then you see the word HELLO. And I did not say anything about a hospital. I said, *87**—turn it up side down and it is L-8, or 'late.' I was telling you I was running late. *123* is 'call me back fast,' you know, like *123*. And *101* means 'no big deal'…or 'this is a snap'—like Math 101!"

"This list I got is no good," said Adam. "Who uses the codes on this list?" He held up the list for Mina to read. She shrugged. Her beeper went off. She looked at the message coming in. "Well," she said. "It has been nice seeing you but I am late for a meeting. I have to go. See you at school!"

Mina turned and ran back the way she came.

"That was some date," said David.

"It turned out to be more beeper talk than date," said Adam. "But I have her number. I will get the codes she knows. I will catch up with her, you will see!"

What Do You Think?

◆ 1. When would it be good to have a beeper with you? Write your answer.

_____

_____

2. When would you rather not have a beeper with you? Write your answer.

_____

_____

Think About the Story

Use Story Words

◆ **Directions:** Look at your list of story words on page 167. Write a story word on each line.

3. place where sick people get help _____

4. what you do with words and letters _____

5. to think _____

6. a word that tells when something happened _____

7. a greeting _____

When Did It Happen?

◆ 8. Write a number from 1 to 5 in front of each event to show when it happened.

_____ David and Adam listen to CDs at the mall.

_____ Mina goes off to a meeting.

_____ Adam and David try to read the beeper message.

_____ Adam thinks the message says "fun," "milk," and "hospital."

_____ Mina tells them what the messages said.

Write Sentences About the Story

◆ **Directions:** Use words from the story to answer these questions.

9. What does Adam use to try to read Mina's message?

_____

_____

10. What does Adam think Mina is trying to tell him?

_____

_____

11. What does the message from Mina say?

_____

_____

What's the Big Idea?

◆ 12. Which sentence tells what the story is mostly about? Write it on the lines.

  a. Beeper codes are a lot of fun, and all the codes are the same.

  b. Mina does not want to meet Adam, so she skips going to the mall.

  c. Adam and Mina meet, but the beeper codes make things tricky.

_____

_____

_____

Letters and Sounds

◆ **Directions:** These words have the short **u** sound. Circle the vowel letter in each word.

  1. us   2. cut

These words have the long **u** sound. Circle the two vowel letters in each word.

  3. use   4. cute

  5. What vowel letter do you see at the end of **use** and **cute**? _____

TIPS: ▸ The letter **u** can stand for the short **u** sound in **us,** or the long **u** sound in **use.**

▸ Words that have the **u**-consonant-**e** pattern usually have the long **u** sound.

◆ **Directions:** Read the words. Circle the words that have the short **u** sound. Draw a line under the words that have the long **u** sound.

Example: (cut)   cute

6. fun	8. flute	10. mutt	12. fuse
7. fume	9. flux	11. mute	13. fuss

◆ **Directions:** Write each word from above in the list where it belongs.

short *u*	long *u*
14. _____	18. _____
15. _____	19. _____
16. _____	20. _____
17. _____	21. _____

◆ **Directions:** Write the letters on the lines. See how many words you can make.

t	d	c	f	pl

22. _____ une	24. _____ ube	26. _____ ume
23. _____ une	25. _____ ube	27. _____ ume

Word Bank

Write each of these story words in the Word Bank at the back of this book.

Story Words

◆ **Directions:** Read each word to yourself. Then say the word out loud. Write the word on the line. Check the box after each step.

love   Read ❑ Say ❑ Write ❑ _____

road   Read ❑ Say ❑ Write ❑ _____

form   Read ❑ Say ❑ Write ❑ _____

letter (let│ter)   Read ❑ Say ❑ Write ❑ _____

around (a│round)   Read ❑ Say ❑ Write ❑ _____

More Word Work

◆ **Directions:** Read each word. Then write the base word and the ending that make it up.

Examples: ripping = rip + ing   liking = like + ing

28. playing   = _____ + _____ ___

29. timing   = _____ + _____ ___

30. rubbed   = _____ + _____

31. listened   = _____ + _____

32. respecting   = _____ + _____

33. slipped   = _____ + _____

◆ **Directions:** Use words from the box to fill in the puzzle.

respect	love	label	letter	road

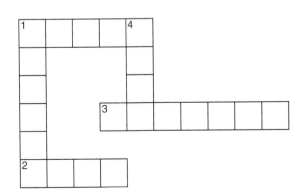

Across
1. what you find on some food products
2. what a bus runs on
3. what you feel when you look up to some one

Down
1. what you can write to a friend
4. liking some one very much

Use What You Know

Numbers can have meanings. Think about these numbers. What do you think of when you see them?

911 _____ ___   411 _____   13 _____ ___

In the next story you will see how some people use numbers to send messages.

NUMBER GAMES

Yes, there is a book that has a long list of beeper message codes. But most kids do not use those codes. There are some codes just about all kids with beepers know. They make up new codes with their friends, too. These are some of the codes kids use on beepers:

07734*	**HELLO** (Hint: Look upside down at the numbers)
14*	**HI** (Again, look at it upside down.)
911	**As quick as you can!** (Like calling 911, this means "no messing around. Act now!")
411	**I need to know something.**
121	**I have to talk to you!** (Can we talk "one-to-one"?)
123	**Call me back as quick as you can.** Some kids use this to say "I miss you." Warning: In one of the beeper books, 123 stands for milk—as in your mom asking your dad to pick some up on the way home.
141	**I get what you are saying.** (I am "one-for-one" with you on that!)
66	**Time to go. Time to hit the road.** (This one comes from the well-known road, U.S. 66.) Warning: In one beeper book, 66 stands for "diapers."
222	**Pick me up after school, OK?**
13	**I am having a very bad day!** (as in unlucky number 13, not the letter M)
30	**Can we drop it now?/ I am finished.** (People who write news use the number 30 to stand for the end of each bit of news.)
2468	**I think you are great.** ("2-4-6-8, I-think-you-are-great!")
13579	**Very odd! / You are odd! / That is odd!** (See, they are all odd numbers.)

80808	**Hugs and kisses** (80808 is as close as you can get to XOXOX on a number pad.)
143	**I love you.** (**I** is a word that has 1 letter, **love** has 4 letters, and **you** has 3 letters.)
17_31707_1*	This is one more way to say "I love you." You have to look at this one up side down. The numbers look a little like the letters.
1040	**You are going to have to pay for this!** (1040 is the number of the form people use for filing their taxes with the IRS.)
5012124	**SORRY** (The numbers look a little like the letters. A 1 and 2 next to each other form the letter R.)
87*	**I am running late!** (Look up side down. L+8 = Late.) Warning: One book codes 87 as fun.
101	**A snap. / Cake. / No problem!** Warning: In one code book, 101 is hospital.
180	**You turned my life around. / I am singing a new tune. / Can we do something new?** (as in a making a 180° turn)

What Do You Think?

◆ 1. Which beeper code do you think is most clever? Why?

_____

_____

Think About the Story

Use Story Words

◆ **Directions:** Look at your list of story words on page 173. Write a story word on each line.

2. rhymes with **sound** _____

3. can mean "to shape" _____

4. A is one. So is **B.** _____

5. a deep feeling _____

6. used for driving on _____

What Is the Code?

◆ **Directions:** Here are some messages you get on your beeper. What do they mean? Use information from the story to write the meanings of the codes.

7. 14*   _____

8. 5012124   _____

9. 87*   _____

10. 30   _____

What Are the Facts?

◆ **Directions:** Write **True** next to each item that is true. Write **False** next to each item that is false.

11. _____ In beeper code, **911** stands for "call the cops."

12. _____ Beeper codes can mean more than one thing.

13. _____ In beeper code, **13** means "I have 13 things to tell you."

14. _____ In beeper code, **411** means "I need to know something."

Write Sentences About the Story

◆ **Directions:** Use words from the story to answer these questions.

15. Do you think beeper codes are a good way to get a message to someone?

_____

_____

16. Which code do you like the best?

_____

_____

17. Which messages would you use the most if you had a beeper?

_____

_____

Chapter 5: Summary of Skills and Strategies

Let's look back at what you learned in Chapter 5.

Letters and Sounds

◆ You learned . . .

  ▸ the letter **o** can stand for the long **o** vowel sound.

  ▸ the letters **e, ee,** and **ea** can stand for the long **e** vowel sound.

  ▸ the letter **i** can stand for the long **i** vowel sound.

  ▸ the letters **ce** can stand for the **s** sound.

  ▸ the letter **u** can stand for the long **u** vowel sound.

Stories and Skills

◆ You learned about . . .

  ▸ some things that are unhealthy for your body.

  ▸ characters who like to use beepers, and how to read beeper messages in code.

◆ You learned . . .

  ▸ how to use what you know to help you understand stories.

  ▸ how to look ahead, or predict, what story characters might do.

Words and Meanings

◆ You learned . . .

  ▸ a lot of new words.

  ▸ when adding **ing** to a word that ends in **e,** drop the **e,** then add the ending.

  ▸ some words sound the same but have different meanings.

  ▸ how to add endings to many words.

The chapter review will give you a chance to show what you have learned.

Part A

Summing It Up: Letters and Sounds

> ▸ The letter **i** can stand for the short **i** sound in **tin** or the long **i** sound in **like**.
> ▸ The letter **o** can stand for the short **o** sound in **not** or the long **o** sound in **note**.
> ▸ The letter **u** can stand for the short **u** sound in **us** or the long **u** sound in **use**.

◆ **Directions:** Read these words. Write each word in the chart where it belongs.

fuse	shop	cute	spin	tone	rope
shine	clip	zone	rip	stop	spine
ripe	drop	cube			

long *i*	short *i*	long *o*	short *o*	long *u*
1. _____	4. _____	7. _____	10. _____	13. _____
2. _____	5. _____	8. _____	11. _____	14. _____
3. _____	6. _____	9. _____	12. _____	15. _____

> ▸ The letter **e** can stand for the short **e** sound in **get** or the long **e** sound in **need**.
> ▸ The letters **e, ee,** and **ea** can stand for long **e**.

◆ **Directions:** Read these words. Write each word in the chart where it belongs.

| ten | weak | men | end |
| she | be | speck | creep |

short *e*	long *e*
16. _____	20. _____
17. _____	21. _____
18. _____	22. _____
19. _____	23. _____

> ▸ The letter **s** is part of many consonant blends. In a word that starts with an **s** blend, you can hear the sound of the **s** and the sound of the other consonant letter.

◆ **Directions:** Read these words. If you can hear the **s** sound and another consonant sound at the beginning, circle the word.

24. speak	27. smoke	30. shut	33. sent
25. snack	28. skip	31. shack	34. sheep
26. shape	29. sleet	32. stick	35. scan

> ▸ Many words end with the letters **ce.** The letters **ce** usually stand for the **s** sound.

◆ **Directions:** Read these words. Circle each word that ends with the **s** sound at the end of **race.**

36. place	38. cute	40. rich	42. must	44. spice
37. such	39. space	41. nice	43. fleece	45. track

Part B

Summing It Up: More Word Work

> ▸ Most words with the CVC pattern have a short vowel sound.
> ▸ Most words with the CVC**e** pattern have a long vowel sound.

◆ **Directions:** Read these words. Write each word in the chart where it belongs.

lip	home	club	spoke	pane	flip
lime	sat	cape	kick	hut	pipe

CVC	CVC*e*
1. _____	7. _____
2. _____	8. _____
3. _____	9. _____
4. _____	10. _____
5. _____	11. _____
6. _____	12. _____

> ‣ You can add **ed** and **ing** to many verbs.
> ‣ When you add **ed** or **ing** to a word with a short vowel sound that ends with a single consonant, double the final consonant. When you add **ed** or **ing** to a word that ends in **e**, drop the **e**.

◆ **Directions:** Add **ed** and **ing** to each word below. Write the new words on the lines.

	add *ed*	add *ing*
13. grin	_____	_____
14. race	_____	_____
15. hope	_____	_____
16. snap	_____	_____
17. hike	_____	_____
18. buzz	_____	_____
19. fan	_____	_____
20. pass	_____	_____

> Some words sound the same, but have different meanings.

◆ **Directions:** Read these word pairs. If the words sound the same, circle **YES**. If they do not sound the same, circle **NO**.

21.	two	to	YES	NO
22.	sea	see	YES	NO
23.	teen	ten	YES	NO
24.	beat	beet	YES	NO
25.	pin	pine	YES	NO
26.	be	bee	YES	NO
27.	form	from	YES	NO
28.	great	grate	YES	NO

Part C

Story Words

◆ **Directions:** On the lines below, write the word from the list that matches each clue.

school	**friend**	**letter**	**talk**
mall	**warning**	**number**	**hospital**
food	**busy**	**hello**	**road**

1. a pal, a chum _____

2. You eat this. _____

3. Speak words. _____

4. Go there to learn. _____

5. Go there to get well. _____

6. Drive on this. _____

7. 5 is one of these. _____

8. Go there to shop. _____

9. first thing to say _____

10. Look out! _____

11. doing many things _____

12. Write this to a friend. _____

◆ **Directions:** On the lines below, write a word from the list to finish each sentence.

cigarette	new	oil	listen
who	love	beeper	around
or	label	figure	after

13. You can read the _____ to find out what is in the box.

14. I want to _____ to the message to find out who called.

15. Each _____ you smoke makes you less fit.

16. That van drips _____ all over the place.

17. *87 and 123 are _____ codes.

18. Do you know _____ used the rake?

19. The letter **c** comes _____ the letter **b.**

20. Is that a river _____ a lake?

21. Abe needs a _____ bike to ride to school.

22. I _____ my new red shoes.

23. This code list will help you _____ out that beeper message.

24. My mom wants to go _____ the world by ship and airplane.

Part D

Think About the Stories

Who Did What?

◆ **Directions:** This list has the names of the people who were in the stories in Chapter 5. Write a name on the line to finish each sentence.

Rob	Brent	David
Clarice	Adam	Mina

1. _____ did not like to inhale cigarette smoke.

2. _____ quit smoking and helped out on the hot line.

3. _____ said, "Stop being such a snob, girl" to try to make his friend smoke a cigarette.

4. _____ was too busy to hang out at the mall.

5. _____ said, "This beeper is my ticket to a date."

6. _____ did not think Adam would get a date.

◆ **Directions:** Read each sentence. If it is true, write **True** on the line. If it is false, write **False** on the line.

7. _____ To learn if a food is OK, you should read the label and do the math.

8. _____ You need all the fat you can eat.

9. _____ In beeper code, 30 means "I think you are great."

10. _____ In beeper code, 80808 is a message you might send to a good friend.

11. _____ A hot line can not help people quit smoking.

12. _____ Tobacco smoke has just two things in it that can make you sick.

13. _____ Some alcohol ads speak to teens.

14. _____ Your body can not use pop, chips, or fast foods as well as it can use good food.

WORD BANK

Chapter 1 Story Words

◆ **Directions:** Write the words from the Story Words section of each lesson. Lesson 1 has been done for you.

LESSON 1   ▶ **The Bungee Jump, Part 1**

I	will
make	no
can	not
a	the
said	bungee
yes	jump
you	fall
may	snap

LESSON 2   ▶ **The Bungee Jump, Part 2**

_____	_____
_____	_____
_____	_____
_____	_____
_____	

LESSON 3   ▶ **The Cave, Part 1**

_____	_____
_____	_____
_____	_____
_____	

Chapter 1 Story Words, continued

LESSON 4 ▶ **The Cave, Part 2**

_____   _____

_____   _____

_____   _____

_____

LESSON 5 ▶ **At the Water Slide, Part 1**

_____   _____

_____   _____

_____   _____

_____

LESSON 6 ▶ **At the Water Slide, Part 2**

_____   _____

_____   _____

_____   _____

Chapter 2 Story Words

◆ **Directions:** Write the words from the Story Words section of each lesson.

LESSON 1 ▶ **Paddle and Roll, Part 1**

_____   _____

_____   _____

_____   _____

_____   _____

_____

WORD BANK

Chapter 2 Story Words, continued

LESSON 2 ▶ **Paddle and Roll, Part 2**

_____   _____

_____   _____

LESSON 3 ▶ **The Track, Part 1**

_____   _____

_____   _____

_____   _____

_____   _____

_____

LESSON 4 ▶ **The Track, Part 2**

_____   _____

_____   _____

_____   _____

LESSON 5 ▶ **Go Climb a Rock**

_____   _____

_____   _____

_____   _____

_____   _____

Chapter 2 Story Words, continued

LESSON 6 ▶ **Big Walls!**

_____   _____

_____   _____

_____   _____

_____   _____

_____

Chapter 3 Story Words

◆ **Directions:** Write the words from the Story Words section of each lesson.

LESSON 1 ▶ **Kick-It-Back**

_____   _____

_____   _____

_____

LESSON 2 ▶ **The Sub Comes Up**

_____   _____

_____   _____

_____   _____

_____

Chapter 3 Story Words, continued

LESSON 3   ▶ **Airplane Quiz**

_____   _____

_____   _____

_____   _____

_____

LESSON 4   ▶ **Night Jump!**

_____   _____

_____   _____

LESSON 5   ▶ **Karate**

_____   _____

_____   _____

_____   _____

_____   _____

LESSON 6   ▶ **Karate Cool**

_____   _____

_____   _____

_____   _____

Chapter 4 Story Words

◆ **Directions:** Write the words from the Story Words
section of each lesson.

LESSON 1 ▶ **In Costume, Part 1**

_____   _____

_____   _____

_____   _____

_____

LESSON 2 ▶ **In Costume, Part 2**

_____   _____

_____   _____

_____   _____

_____   _____

_____

LESSON 3 ▶ **America's Biggest and Baddest Rides**

_____   _____

_____   _____

LESSON 4 ▶ **Girls Send Plastics Into Space**

_____   _____

_____   _____

_____   _____

_____   _____

Chapter 4 Story Words, continued

LESSON 5 ▶ **Take It by Skate, Part 1**

_____ _____

_____ _____

_____ _____

_____

LESSON 6 ▶ **Take It by Skate, Part 1**

_____ _____

_____ _____

_____ _____

Chapter 5 Story Words

◆ **Directions:** Write the words from the Story Words section of each lesson.

LESSON 1 ▶ **Up in Smoke, Part 1**

_____ _____

_____ _____

_____ _____

_____

LESSON 2 ▶ **Up in Smoke, Part 2**

_____ _____

_____ _____

_____ _____

_____

Chapter 5 Story Words, continued

LESSON 3 ▶ **What Are You Putting in Your Body?**

_____ _____

_____ _____

_____ _____

_____ _____

_____

LESSON 4 ▶ **Beep Me! Part 1**

_____ _____

_____ _____

_____ _____

LESSON 5 ▶ **Beep Me! Part 2**

_____ _____

_____ _____

_____

LESSON 6 ▶ **Number Games**

_____ _____

_____ _____

_____